Child,
Please

Child, Please

Please

How Mama's Old-School Lessons

Helped Me Check Myself

before I Wrecked Myself

Ylonda Gault Caviness

JEREMY P. TARCHER / PENGUIN

an imprint of Penguin Random House • New York

JEREMY P. TARCHER/PENGUIN
An imprint of Penguin Random House LLC
375 Hudson Street
New York, New York 10014

Most Tarcher/Penguin books are available at special quantity discounts for bulk
purchase for sales promotions, premiums, fund-raising, and educational needs.
Special books or book excerpts also can be created to fit specific needs. For details,
write: SpecialMarkets@penguinrandomhouse.com.

ISBN 978-0-399-16996-0

Printed in the United States of America
1   3   5   7   9   10   8   6   4   2

Book design by Gretchen Achilles

Some names and identifying characteristics have been
changed to protect the privacy of the individuals involved.

Contents

Child, Please

Often the Look was not particularly stern. Nor scary. In fact, Mama's Look was eerily subtle on its surface. The pain danced on the edges—dangerously jagged, sharp points skirting the axis of her wan expression. It was clear, even to a young child, that just beyond the thin layer of restraint lay a machete-like stab of pure, unadulterated, extra-strength INDIFFERENCE.

The Look rode shotgun with an audible sigh—weary and deep. A pointed and distinctive breath dripping heavily with enough annoyance and discontent to let you know Mama was so, so sick and tired of your very existence in that moment. On the exhale, an assiduous listener—like myself—might strain to make out muffled syllables cloaked under exasperated huffs. That was when her simmering aggravation was given voice—ever so faintly. Soft as a whisper, but laced with aversion, the words escaped her pursed lips: *"Child, please . . ."*

In other words, "Go someplace and sit down." *Child, please* said, "Get out of my face." It meant, "You don't even warrant the energy it would take to go off on your behind." For Mama, *Child, please* was also shorthand for "I'm going to smoke me a cigarette and I want nothing to do with your foolishness." At that, she'd softly turn on her heel for a cutting exit. Pure theater. Had we owned velvet curtains they'd have closed dramatically then and there.

We did not.

For the next ten minutes or so I felt like a bothersome speck of lint on her black bell-bottom pants. Certainly there is an expert out there right now decrying the near-abusive blow to my self-esteem. But don't give me that noise about kids' confidence. I'm not trying to hear it. In most households these days, the children could stand to be knocked down a notch or two. Mama's *Child, please* packed a powerful and dramatic lesson. She was tone deaf, but her message held poetic rhythms, like the Queen of Soul chirping: *R-E-S-P-E-C-T, find out what it means to me!* Her *Child, please* was all about the boundaries Mama expected us kids to recognize. In an instant—before she uttered a sound, or even heaved in exasperation—I knew I'd crossed an indelible line.

My own kids? Hmmm . . . they sort of get the whole

boundary thing, but it's not quite as reflexive as I'd like. For example, they sometimes butt into grown folks' conversation—as modern children are wont to do. And then have the nerve to give me a look of puppy-dog confusion when I call them on it. I am forced to remind them: "Dude, I dared not even look in my mother's direction when she was talking to her friends; your head is jogging back and forth like you're checking a match at Arthur Ashe Stadium." Honestly, they are better than most. Usually they *try* to control themselves, but the fact is, kids today harbor the illusion that they are our equals. They fancy themselves smarter, shorter adults—less keys and credit cards.

Back in the day, mothers didn't suffer the mess we put up with now. Of course, the culture as a whole was far more stringent. No one I knew was unfamiliar with the sting of a belt across their backside. Beyond that, though, we didn't take our parents' attention—or their affection—for granted.

I, for one, wanted Mama's approval. And it was clearly a prize not easily won. Mama loved us. Of that my siblings and I had no doubt. But we also knew she wasn't necessarily *in* love with us—at least not just because.

There was no cheering our descent down the slide. She didn't hang with clusters of moms at the playground like infatuated groupie spectators squealing from the stands.

Nor did she gush over our every stick figure drawing and plaster them all over the house. Like everyone else's mother, Mama was happy and sufficiently enthused when we won a spelling bee or some such achievement, but she wasn't hanging on our words or asking, "You okay?" all the time. I'm pretty sure we took up no more of her energy than was necessary. Without saying so, she let us know we kids could sometimes rock her world, but we couldn't *be* her world.

That's why Mama observes my generation of mothers with befuddled amusement. She concedes, of course, that times have changed: We mothers have more complicated lives and our kids face far more dangers. Still, the self-flagellating, all-consuming obsession to raise a child in a fashion akin to a recipe-perfect soufflé is mind-blowing to her. And it's no wonder. Mothering as an extreme sport is a world far removed from her own sensibilities. When I stop to think about how my friends and I live, here are just some of the ways we differ from old-school motherhood:

- Mama didn't run out of the house—as I often do—wearing ill-fitting clothes and no lipstick.
- She didn't fret about how well I did in school, how easily I made friends, or how good I was in music lessons. (Wait . . . Oh, that's right. I didn't have music lessons.)

- Mama never hired a babysitter.
- She didn't know of, consider, or care about child-friendly explanations for life's difficulties. "Well. Your uncle Dave decided to blow his brains out" sufficed.
- She never let our displeasure get in the way of her good time, dancing the Funky Chicken till her legs tired, oblivious to our tears from embarrassment.
- Mama didn't pencil in "girlfriend time"; she relished hours-long, impromptu chat fests whenever Aunt San or Sugar decided to drop by the house.
- She threw parties at the drop of a hat and took full advantage of our free labor, putting us to work making the deviled eggs and cream cheese celery sticks. (We loved every minute—especially those times Jimmy Mo' got drunk.)
- She seldom took our side in a misunderstanding or report of misconduct. If a neighbor, a teacher, or any other grown-up accused us of wrongdoing, we were presumed guilty until proven innocent.
- Mama never played shrink. Her lips never formed words like "Tell me about it" or "How did that make you feel?"
- Mama wasn't studying us.

As kids we accepted this reality. It was neither harsh nor troubling; rather, it seemed the natural order of things. As a child you knew you didn't matter all that much in the grown-up world. If you lay bleeding, someone would probably attend to you. And if you acted out, you definitely commanded notice. But, by and large, grown-ups were not studying kids. I don't mean the academic studying that leads to a weird analysis, like "SpongeBob linked to attention deficits" or "Daycare increases aggression in kids." In southern black parlance, *studying* means "paying attention to." And lest my siblings and I get any fleeting misapprehension that we figured into the larger scheme of things, Mama was quick to remind us: "Child, I am *not* studying you!"

As any fool could see, Mama had the whole motherhood thing down to a science. Her ship was tight—so tight she reminded us almost daily, "I'm the captain; you're the crew."

Through the lens of modern parenting, Mama's ways may seem to border on neglect—given our national obsession with everything child-related. But they worked. The old-fashioned "not studying you" method fostered independence, self-reliance, and a generation of thinkers and doers—running circles around our newfangled, expert concepts.

Mama had balance—without really even trying—and without a gaggle of contrived self-help tips telling her how to get it. She and her friends didn't sit around and gab about balance between drags on their cigarettes, saying, "Girrrl, I gotta get me some balance!" They didn't wonder if they spent enough quality time with us kids. And they damn sure weren't pressed about finding "me time." The very concept would've sent them into howling spasms of laughter.

"Girl, it's *all* 'me time'! Who else's time is it gon' be?"

People say I'm a lot like Mama. Family and friends have always said I got her smile, her high forehead and cheek-bones. Growing up, I was never able to see what they saw. I figured we looked like we were related, but I never grasped the "your-mama-spit-you-out!" so obvious to the outside world. But now, in my forties, I finally get it. In fact, there are days when a mirror catches me by surprise and I see her staring back at me. Her mouth. Her stance.

But beyond the physical markers, there are glimpses of her Mama-ness slowly creeping up on me. It is more palpable—for some reason—now than ever before. Lord knows, my kids have spent the better part of their short lives trying to work my last good nerve. It's their job, I tell myself. No need to find the just-right response: Is this a teachable moment? Do I take away a privilege? Do I try to empathize?

No. I just take a good, long breath . . . *Child, please.*

Child,
Please

CHAPTER ONE

Get Ready, You Mutha, for the Big Payback

H*iiii. How Ahhh Youuu? Please picka your cullaaa!"*
How sweet the sound of the Korean ladies at
Seven Nails. I know the same rote greeting is showered
upon every customer who walks in. Still, something about
the saccharine-dipped chorus tickles me. It's nice to know
that even midweek, early in the afternoon, the trademark
smiles and singsong pleasantries of my trusted nail ladies
do not waver. At thirty-nine-and-a-half weeks pregnant I
had no business waddling down Seventh Avenue, risking
life and limb in the treacherous postnap rush of Park Slope
stroller traffic. It's true that some experts advise a pre-
labor enema, but *What to Expect When You're Expecting*
said nary a word about trim cuticles and fresh shellac.

To my mind a mani-pedi made perfect sense. Any
day now, a mess of amniotic fluid could be running down
my inner thighs like hot pee. My hormone-charged imag-

ination found me sopping it up in the aisles of Duane Reade or on the D train, while my fellow commuters pretended to look away. In the event of some horrifically humiliating scenario, a nice coat of Ballet Slippers could make the whole experience a little more, you know, classy.

Besides, I knew I was having a girl and she'd likely appreciate this ladylike gesture. I'd decided to call her Chloe. I liked that Chloe had played a brief but prominent role in the New Testament. Chloe was also Toni Morrison's given name. Clearly, mine would be no simple child.

We were tight—my soon-to-be firstborn and me. We'd been involved in some pretty intense heart-to-hearts since around week twenty-two of my pregnancy. That was when I found out that—despite virtually every casual observer's comments—I was having a girl. Up until then I had come to believe the extremely vocal group of Midtown Manhattan construction workers who saw it as their appointed duty to track the spread of my butt cheeks and make their gender predictions accordingly. I was thoroughly disgusted by the fact that not even the sanctity of impending motherhood got in the way of their vulgarity. But at the same time, I thought the brutes might know a thing or two. Several of the hard hats yelled things like, "Yo, Mommy . . . You lookin' *goooood*, baby; that's a boy seed up in there." Grandmotherly types concurred. Sizing up the shape and positioning of my belly with knowing looks, they'd say, "I hope you've got your boy names picked out."

Then came the ultrasound—which revealed not even a shadow of dangly little male parts. I was "scurred" as an ice-grilled Dirty South gangster rapper. I lay stunned on that ultrasound table for a good while, taking it in. How in the world was I supposed to usher that sketchy little unborn blob on the screen into full-grown Black Womanhood?

I didn't fear actually giving birth. For some reason, I figured that would be the easy part. Of course, no visibly pregnant woman is safe from the onslaught of delivery horror stories that greet you at every turn. On occasion, these dramatic miniseries of seventy-two-hour labors and emergency C-sections did rattle me a bit. But despite a reigning consensus that my hips were too narrow for a baby to slide forth, I had a gut feeling things would go smoothly.

My hunch was confirmed when my pregnancy entered its home stretch; I was waiting for the crosstown bus on my way home from a prenatal visit. (I didn't know then that it would be my last office check-in.) My eye caught a kindly black woman staring at me and smiling. She asked if I was ready—gesturing toward my oversized midsection. I laughed. "Not even," and told her about my unpacked hospital bag and still-unbought baby gear. She smiled and said, "Never mind all that, baby girl. Get yourself right."

I sensed that maybe the small talk was a ruse and she was about to start ranting, "REPENT! REPENT!" like the wild Bible thumpers in Times Square. But she just kept smiling. I suppose I was visibly confused. She said, "God made you a woman, didn't he?" I nodded and she whispered, "Relax . . . let it do what it do."

Maybe that's why I was bold enough (or stupid enough) to duckwalk it to the nail salon in my condition. In my own defense, though, I thought I had a lot of time to kill. Hours before setting out for Seven Nails, I'd called my doctor because Chloe was waging quiet mortal combat all up in my nether regions. I had no way of knowing what back labor felt like, but let me just say that Chloe's sharp movements gave stark illumination to the term *ass whooping*.

Dr. Shaun Biggers was my OB/GYN but could well have been one of my best girlfriends. We vibed like that. During my last visit she kept going on and on about how my cervix was "nicely effacing." I accepted the compliments (*Go cervix! Go cervix!*) with no real understanding of what the heck she meant. That afternoon when she answered my page, I gave her an efficient and comprehensive report of everything going on "down there," but I could tell she was not moved. In fact, it seemed as though my litany of earth-shattering vaginal events was boring her. In a kind and professional voice, she suggested that—this being my first pregnancy and all—I might be in this "pre-labor" state for days. My heart of hearts told me otherwise, but she summarily announced that she and her girlfriends were heading out to see *How Stella Got Her Groove Back* that night. She was too nice to actually articulate the words, but the sister-girl tone of her voice said, *and don't bother me with no nonsense.* She then ordered me to "chill." Seven Nails beckoned.

Initially things at the salon went well, but as I attempted to transfer my wide body from the pedicure station—with its raised platform and gargantuan chairs—I felt weak and nauseated. I tried to play it cool. As the Nail Salon Lady began the ritualistic lotion massage, a sharp spasm pierced my back through to the left side of my abdomen. I quickly waved my hands—like a white flag—and announced: "I think I'm kind of in labor." I spoke quietly, hoping that for the remainder of the session it would be our little secret.

No such luck. If the Nail Salon Ladies were a sweet girl group at the start of my visit, they were now elevated to Brooklyn Tabernacle proportions. Only I'd clearly thrown them off their rhythm. They broke out in a frenzied kind of jazz improv routine, filled with scats and such. This new tune was not so melodic as their usual repertoire. After just a couple of moments the contraction passed. And eager to restore some sense of calm, I whispered: "Skip the second coat; I should get going."

That must've been music to *their* ears. With choreographed precision the Nail Salon Ladies went all triage on me—while one painted my right hand a colleague painted the left and another positioned a small fan at my freshly painted toes. Within ten minutes I was out of there—trudging through the crowded streets of Park Slope, desperate for the cool comfort of my living room sofa.

Did I mention that it was mid-August? For the record, let me just say that the rising mercury and overall hazy-hot-humid stench of New York City does not mix well with labor or the symptoms that usually accompany it. I was drenched with sweat soaking right down to the ample, Big Mama drawers I'd grown so fond of during these last several weeks of swollenness. My fleshy thighs—the beneficiaries of at least half of my pregnancy weight gain—were fighting again, hitting each other in a tit-for-tat scuffle so fierce I could feel the chafing. And a slimy sour cast had begun to well up in my mouth as a reminder that my morning's breakfast wanted out.

The Great Trek finally ended as I got inside our apartment and headed straight for the shower, where I stood, as best I could stand, under the streaming water for thirty minutes or thirty hours—I'm not sure which. Still sweltering and light-headed, I opted to forgo the whole towel routine—air-drying myself instead by lying on the cold tile floor. That was where Mark found me, looking like a beached whale from a tearjerker special on Discovery Channel, when he came home from work.

In hindsight, I can appreciate how scary it must've been for him. But I was not in my right mind. And when he started to panic, insisting that we go to the hospital, I lost it. I really went off. "I. AM. JUST. CHILLING!" I yelled.

He was all in a tizzy. And even though I didn't get up off the floor (I swear, the cool tiles felt like heaven in that moment), I could hear him pacing the length of the apartment.

I guess my "just chilling" explanation was not all that convincing. He kept going back and forth, forth and back—the percussion of Johnston & Murphy vibrating to shattering effects from my eardrums to my kidneys. Right about the time he rounded the hallway for the umpteenth time, I about lost my mind! (On background, just so you know, I had asked the man to take off his shoes in the house since I met him—just because I think that's what people in civilized society ought to do. Was it really too much to ask?) Here I am in labor and I'm forced to deal with his trifling mess. I began screaming and screaming, "TAKE. OFF. YOUR. SHOES!" There was some cussing tossed in there as well, but I'll spare you the coarse details.

Between a baby mercilessly beating upon all my organs and a husband breaking the sound barrier, I couldn't get an ounce of calm. Maybe a trip to New York Presbyterian Hospital would do me good. "Let's go," I said finally.

Mark grew a little more at ease once I agreed to get up off the floor and leave the house peaceably. The fact that it was nearly impossible to actually sit my behind on the car seat struck me as just another symptom of early labor. So I went yogi; I hoisted my butt up—in a sort of lifted lotus pose—using my arms to support my body weight the entire way from Brooklyn to the Upper East Side. Along the arduous trip up the FDR, the contractions were intensifying and I braced myself against the potholes relentlessly abusing my cervix.

To my great relief, we arrived in fairly short order. But, lo and behold, somewhere on the FDR, Mark had found his labor-coach mojo. As we tried to extract my body from the car, he started prattling on in trainer-speak: "You're doing great, babe." "You're almost there." I know the intent was to encourage me, but it was working my last nerve. Big-time. Why on earth did he choose this moment to relive his college football days? The rah-rah voice? Cheering, even—"Yes! You can do it!" I do wish I could've been more kind. He meant well. But this was not first-and-goal and I was not some backup quarterback coming off the bench. I didn't want to go off in public, but everybody knows that times like this bring out the evil in a sister! It took all I had not to utter the string of expletives pushing against my lips.

Meanwhile, down at my hips, Chloe was also pressing. Hard. Fortunately, my child did not need a cheering section to get her into the end zone. Once I got my whalelike hips up to the labor and delivery table, come to find out, I was dilated nearly nine centimeters, a medical way of saying "Homegirl was *ret tuh* go!"

To this day, I can't be sure if Mark called this play or what. But he and a burly nurse had gone into a tag-team formation of sorts just as I began to push—each standing on either side of me. With all the grace and decorum of Fred Flintstone grabbing a brontosaurus leg, the nurse held up one thigh and Mark the other (luckily I'd had a thorough bikini wax days prior, slightly mitigating the beastly effect of the whole event). Somehow it all worked and Chloe arrived on the scene smoothly, probably eager to witness the circus for herself (to this day, she loves a drama).

And there she was. Ta-da!

I know I have no right to complain. Despite myself I'd had a safe and trauma-free childbirth experience. I mean, I'd become a mom in less time than it takes to get in and out of the Flatbush Avenue DMV and survive the surly workers who all but spit in your face. Here she was. Yessir, she was born all right. A sight to behold. Really, in her own special way, she was beautiful-ish.

Let me explain . . . She had a really cute little mouth and lots of hair. I guess I was just expecting something—well, different. Mama says I was a big baby. As my in-laws tell it, Mark clocked in at around eight pounds. Although I worked out during the pregnancy, I denied myself nary a French fry. So why in God's name did my loin fruit, born only four days shy of her late-summer due date, pop out looking like the spawn of Posh Beckham?

Chloe weighed a little over five and a half pounds. Old black folks from down South (and not-so-old ones up North) had a name for her physical frailty. She was a "po' chile." Yes, my new baby was freakishly scrawny—UNICEF-worthy, even. Probably she would've been a hit on the late-night charity infomercial circuit—the kind Sally Struthers could just eat up. When the doctor placed her naked boniness on my chest on that sticky-hot Tuesday night of August eighteenth, Chloe's entire being seemed nothing but pupil, round near-black planes bulging from a teensy little head. "Where did this Chihuahua-looking-wannabe-human creature come from?" I wondered.

As she shivered and bawled, Chloe's gaze was fixed on me—eyeing me with an intent defying her minutes-old entry into the world. It lasted for all of twenty seconds; I remember the countenance to this day as she lay there staring up at me like *I* was the miracle. If it was not love at first sight, it was at the very least penetrating intrigue.

Before too long, though, the kid had me. Once they wiped off some of the blood and slime and she lay on my chest—still bawling, at volume levels of a baby twice her size—I could feel the Love Jones coming on. And I knew life could not get any better than that moment. To this day, I remember that awestruck feeling. And once in a while, Chloe still can make my heart skip a beat. I guess that's why she's my favorite child. But please don't tell anyone, because mothers are really not supposed to say such things.

Despite appearances, her Apgar score was good and they assured me she was in prime shape. I say "they" because Dr. Biggers never did make it. I guess the chiseled hotness of Taye Diggs (in Technicolor, no less) proved too much to resist. Who could be mad at that?

Mom and baby had managed just fine. I was no worse for wear and Chloe was as hearty as any newborn in the nursery—a couple of L.B.s short of bouncy, but healthy just the same.

The next morning she was starting to "cute up" a bit. But I would not be satisfied until I got her to fill out. The prospects did not look good. I'd read every morsel of information on breast-feeding, but it seemed to me— although she was less than twelve hours old—Chloe already had attitude. Girlfriend wanted to call all the shots, like it was her world and I was just a squirrel. The books laid out all the steps and I followed them. I was doing what I was supposed to do, but this chick clearly had a rebel streak in her pint-sized self. It was as though she were saying, *House Party* style: "Hold up . . . Wait a minute!"

Chloe was determined to make her own latch-on rules, despite my attempts to encourage her otherwise. I couldn't tell if she was getting any milk at all. But the raw state of my itty-bitty titties told me that this child was doing more gnawing than nursing.

Is this normal? I wondered. The lactation expert said what I'd pretty much surmised on my first full day of motherhood: Breast-feeding is natural, but—like Big Daddy Kane's pimpin'—it sho' ain't easy. Some babies require more nudging than others. She talked about the "rooting" reflex and how some babies don't automatically know how to latch on—they have to be coaxed, directed even.

It was all very troubling. I mean, clearly, Chloe was as bright as other newborns in the nursery. Right? Would she lag in other ways too? Would she roll over? Learn the ABC song? Go to college?

A bit of my mama began to kick in. "This calls for some tough love," I thought. I tried holding Chloe's tiny mouth open wider so she'd latch on the way babies are supposed to. But when she started to fuss and cry, I punked out. At the next feeding I tried gently pushing the breast into her mouth. But that didn't quite work out either. She'd just clamp her gums down tight on any piece of flesh she could—sending daggerlike pains to every nerve ending in my racked body.

In my pre-delivery fantasies, I saw myself nursing my new baby and looking like one of those blissed-out magazine cover models in my OB/GYN's waiting room. Mama had made no secret of the fact that breast was not best in her book. So I wanted her to see how wonderful it would be. Hardly. Mama would soon arrive and nursing was not fun yet.

I needn't have fretted. Seeing Chloe made Mama as happy as I'd ever seen her in my entire life. So happy, in fact, she'd promptly forgotten I was in the room. Heaven only knows where her thoughts took her as she stared at this newborn product of her. Did she wish her own mother were alive to share this bliss? Did she feel surprised or overwhelmed by the surge of love her heart was pouring out onto this child? Did she have just a tinge of longing for the maternal bond she had never experienced?

After she held Chloe for what seemed like several days, she handed her off to the nurse and—still beaming— looked to me and said, "You look good, baby." I couldn't possibly have looked all that good. To a mother I suppose I did. Mama had said those four words with frequency my whole life.

But now, as an adult, I was beginning to learn that they were like a code language for Mama. I would hear them after I'd suffered my first miscarriage. Again, after the second, and on several other occasions when Mama's heart was too full to elaborate.

They were as close as she could get to utterances that sounded anything like:

- This is a wonderful/difficult moment.
- I feel (fill in the blank) proud/touched/sad/delighted/ unsettled/a brew of happiness and yearning.
- How do you feel?

It was all good, though. While she was not always easy to read, today Mama's eyes told me that, without a doubt, she was mostly experiencing unbridled joy. She looked on curiously as I fumbled through another clumsy breast-feeding session. Then, as only a mother can, she began asking a long series of well-meaning—and maddening—questions: "Is she getting anything?" "How do you know how many ounces?" "You sure you don't want to pack this formula and take it home?" "You know it's free, right?"

By the time we left the hospital, Chloe had invented her own brand of nursing, quite unlike anything I'd read about in the baby books and nowhere near the steps laid out by the lactating geniuses on staff. And Mama tried her level best not to judge, which was hard—given that there didn't seem to be all that much for her to do during Chloe's first few days of life.

CHAPTER TWO

Ain't It Funky Now?

Mama didn't like what I fed the baby. *Give that child a bottle and call it a day.*

Mama didn't like *when* I fed the baby. *It's every four hours—not every whenever.*

She didn't like "doctor-recommended" advice. *I guess common sense isn't common at all.*

She said I didn't swaddle the baby right. *Wrap. Tuck. Fold. Simple.*

I held the baby wrong too: My grip was supposed to be tight. *I can just look at that poor child and tell she's uncomfortable.*

And why the hell was I holding the baby so much anyway? According to Mama, I carried her too much. Fussed too much. Thought too much. Read too much. Bought too much.

Mama was too much.

In hindsight I should've known we might butt heads. Mama and I hadn't spent concentrated, 24/7 time together since I was a child. Back then, she said I could be anything I wanted to be. I believed her.

After high school, I left the cold, gritty gray of Buffalo for Northwestern University outside Chicago—the only school I'd applied to. My grades, SAT scores, and essay were pretty good. Not great. Probably I'd willed myself out of Buffalo, into the Medill School of Journalism. For my entire adult life, Mama and I were separated by hundreds of miles. She liked visiting me in Chicago. When I moved East, she *loved* visiting me in New York. Between visits, we talked on the phone all the time. Shared secrets. Laughed. I liked to think we were close despite the distance.

On an extraordinarily pleasing August day—clear skies with a southerly wind—we brought the baby home to the Park Slope apartment my husband had renovated himself. Three bedrooms, plus outdoor space. By city standards, it was palatial. With Mama in my cozy space of new motherhood, the walls began to close in upon me. Her scrutiny lurked in every room, every nook and cranny. I soon learned I had not only failed Baby Basics, but I had a slew of heretofore undiscovered shortcomings that needed her urgent attention.

- Mama said I was not cleaning our wood floors properly. Damp mopping with vinegar was apparently the only way to go.
- Mama said I needed to "do something" with my hair.
- Mama said I should encourage my husband more often—praise him for changing a diaper, cleaning spit-up, and performing virtually every act of caregiving he bestowed upon the creature born of DNA he'd so willingly provided.
- Mama said I should sleep when the baby slept—unless of course she sent me on an errand or two.
- Mama said that from the looks of my still-bulging belly, the doctors had maybe forgotten to deliver the baby's hidden twin. She cracked herself up with that one.

I have no scientific proof, but I am pretty sure that in most families a new baby is a sweetly moving experience, rich in promise and emotion. I suppose Mama felt some of that. Deep down. Right now, though, there was no time for snotty-nosed sentiment. This was all business. The feeding schedules, bedtime rituals, and other baby regulations required her utmost attention and my meticulous compliance—postnatal hormones, sleep deprivation, and new-mom vulnerability be damned.

We had a baby to raise. So what if the poor li'l thing couldn't yet see straight and her tissue-paper-thin skin still peeled daily. Rules were rules. And they were made to be followed. Naptime was naptime. Period. Only a fool would risk a child's total ruination by jumping up whenever she cried. Not on Mama's watch. As she declared with dark foreboding on more than one occasion: "What you do at six weeks, you'll do at sixteen!" Usually this dire warning was accompanied by a raised eyebrow—her left, which was code for *Go ahead with your fool self. Don't act like I never told you.*

Mama had a plan to whip me into shape but good. She would make a mama out of me if it killed us. It nearly did.

Once while I nursed my baby in the quiet stillness of our marital bed, Mama came in to pull my tiny newborn infant off my swollen breast—oblivious to the near-industrial-strength powers of a baby's suction-cup grip: "C'mon now . . . Let go. It's bath time," she cloyingly sang in a newly acquired grandmother lilt. When her grandchild wailed, Mama would simply sing louder, often dropping a passive-aggressive comment (in baby talk, of course) on her way out—something like, "Thank you, Grandma. Silly mommy doesn't hold me right."

Even when Mama left me to my own devices with the baby (a rarity), her judgments echoed in my head, largely because I could hear her in the next room. Mama always enjoyed gossip with her friends—"Sugar" and a core group of two or three women were like "other mothers" to my siblings and me. They called frequently to check on me. Mere seconds after gushing with grandma pride, Mama would start in. Born lacking the filter mechanism that keeps most humans from disgorging any and all brain wave activities, Mama felt she ought to share her observations of my amateurish maternal performance with *everyone*. In fact, she delighted in these chat fests.

"*Giirrrrrl* . . . Bless her heart. She's trying," Mama would crow—bemused as though I were a cute toddler attempting some grown-up feat. "Talking 'bout what the doctor said and what the book said . . . I told her, 'Look, I raised three children. . . .'" Technically, I suppose it was not gossip. Mama was basically repeating what she'd been telling me—albeit with more gleeful jeering than instruction. The conversations were always laced with boisterous laughter on her part and *tsk-tut* headshaking. She added the occasional "*Hmph*" for high effect, punctuated by the "Uuuuuh-huh" and "Okay?" utterances without which an exchange between some black women would not be complete. Even more than all her arbitrary rules, these telephone exchanges grew old quickly.

A few times I'd considered calling her out on this behavior—giving Mama a piece of my mind. "I am a grown-ass woman," I wanted to blast, "not the butt of your amusement." But then I barely had enough energy to shower and brush my teeth. And you'd have to know Mama to understand what a futile exercise an open, heart-felt dialogue would be. She would accuse me of being overly sensitive. Very likely, the word *silly* would pass her lips. And, in the end, she'd laugh and give me a love tap on the forehead. To Mama's way of thinking, there was no downside to speaking her mind—no matter how hurtful. Any upset would be way beyond her comprehension. She'd argue—defiantly—"Look, I was just saying. . . ."

That was about the closest she'd come to any kind of apology. It was hard to deal with. But for nearly sixty years, Mama had practiced separating herself from emotions—beginning, I suppose, with the onslaught of shame and ridicule she endured from The Stepmother, who taunted her with insults like "You so black and ugly" and "You ain't shit." Mama's own mother died when she was just three years old. A few years later, her dad—my grandfa-ther, Papa—remarried an excruciatingly miserable woman who brought several of her own children to the marriage: light-skinned with "white people" hair. No telling who their daddy was or where he was. Soon after, Mama's three sisters left Alabama for Mississippi—leaving her and her brother Dave behind, for some reason. Mama seldom spoke about it; what few sketches of her childhood I had came from family friends and relatives, not Mama herself.

Asking questions yielded little or nothing because the "past is the past," as Mama would always say; "no sense dredging it up." What hurt her more than The Stepmother's cruelty, I think, was Papa's inability or refusal to recognize it. He worked for the railroad and was in and out of town frequently. When he was home, he tried in his own way to give Mama and her brother extra love and attention. That usually meant slipping them treats and spare cash. Uncle Dave happily accepted, while Mama on the other hand stubbornly refused—resentful that he couldn't or wouldn't stand up to his wife.

If she was detached from her own feelings, Mama couldn't really manage to put much stock in anyone else's. It's not like I have a psychology degree. But I tell myself that, partly because I believe it to be true and partly because I need it to be.

Mama meant well. Lord knows she did.

I think she desperately needed to keep life simple and on her terms. To her mind, there were only two ways of doing things: her way and the wrong way. Take your pick. She saw it as her appointed duty to point out the error of your ways at every opportunity—to keep you from going out into the world "half-ass backward." As my luck would have it, having Mama on hand for this protracted visit gave her plenty of time to right my wrongs.

See, some parents dish out tough love when it is needed.

Tough love was pretty much the only love Mama knew. Like her coffee, it was strong, black, and intense at every turn. For more than thirty years, I'd stood witness to Mama's love, running deep and hard. Its unwavering nature was fitting. Mama lived in a cut-and-dried, black-and-white world that left little or no room for *almosts*. As my father would learn nine years into their marriage, Mama's love was inherently unforgiving. I now know that it was not because she was so strong, but because she was delicate. Dad had his own ghosts—stories he didn't tell or joke about. Like his mother up and leaving the South Carolina home she'd made with my grandfather and their six young children for a new life up North. He didn't talk about how he subsisted on little food and no education to speak of as a boy. How much he wanted to be loved or how badly he needed to be taken care of. It's little wonder that he took up with women all around town and squandered his paycheck—to the point where his penchant for three-piece suits, pocket watches, and the like left his wife and kids groping around with the lights out and eating canned pork-and-beans.

Frailty was not an option for those who loved Mama. She needed you to buck up—for your own good. It may have felt unrelentingly cold, but Mama was only trying to *help* you when she tore you down. I knew that. Love, in the only form she knew, led her to this boot-camp style of nurturing. It was preparation for all the difficulties she knew you'd face.

Sure, I wanted a little tenderness, but Mama grew up in Birmingham with the scourge of Jim Crow outside her door—blocks away from the famous 16th Street Baptist Church bombing that killed four little girls in 1963. And there was little safety in her home with The Stepmother, who barely fed her, let alone loved her.

Mama didn't do tender. From Mama, you got the love you needed, not the love you wanted.

It was better this way. Life could chew you up and spit you out. And, as Mama often reminded my siblings and me, "Crying about it won't do any good." More than its stark lens, the hardest thing to accept about Mama's strong love was this: Usually she was right.

Like the time in third grade when I returned home from the first day at my new school—one of the six I attended from kindergarten to eighth grade. It had been a good day and I excitedly shared stories about my new friends. There was Orlando with the funny accent who was clearly smitten with me. There was a girl named Yolanda—the first with my name that I'd met in my whole life, despite the odd spelling. At recess, tons of kids invited me to play. Even the nuns seemed cool. This was going to be one great school.

After letting me babble on and on while she nodded

obligingly, Mama turned to look me straight in the eye and said matter-of-factly: "These kids are not your friends—until they prove it. And most of them never will." When I looked up at her, visibly shaken, she took the time to break things down to my eight-year-old level, something she seldom did, so I knew this had to be important: "A friend is not a person who is nice to you. A friend is someone who is there for you."

See? That's what I'm talking about. No matter how Mama's words cut, you had to respect her gangster.

I knew well Mama's straight-no-chaser, brown-juice tongue. I knew her implacable standards. I could sometimes remember, in vivid detail, nights when she woke my siblings and me in the middle of the night to address a mediocre chore performance: "You call that floor clean? Mop it till you get it right!" I knew that, like the James Brown song, Mama didn't take no mess!

What I hadn't counted on was the idea that by giving birth and mothering my baby I could somehow, once again, fall short. Call me crazy, but I thought Mama would be pleased with me. I thought—hoped—she would appreciate (maybe even respect?) the woman I'd become. I'd borne her first grandchild, after all. And she'd waited a long time. Not that she minded or complained, because I'd done this baby thing the "right" way: finished school, gotten married. Not like some of her friends' daughters who had produced "illegitimate" kids.

There were many, many things Mama was adamantly against: streaked windows, dingy underwear, ashy knees and elbows, stained tile grout, and toilet rings among them. But "bastards" were near the top of the list. She'd drilled into my sister and me (my brother too, for that matter) that we were not to bring home any bastard babies. She'd have no part of it. My sister and I were ordered to keep our panties up and our dresses down. Period. She reminded us constantly that "I've raised my children. I have no plans to raise yours. If you want to have sex and act all grown, you best get the hell up out of here."

Maybe it was pregnancy brain, but in the weeks leading up to Mama's arrival I had apparently erased all traces of history and reality. I somehow expected Grandma-Mama to be totally different from Mama-Mama. My hormones were definitely messing up my head; they had me all sappy and confused. When I was barely three months along, I began weeping over flowery Summer's Eve commercials (not the newer ones with talking vajayjays; I'm talking circa 1998 grassy meadows). I'd become all melancholy and goofy. Could a mere swollen belly turn me into Boo Boo the Fool? Something had taken over, and I had this Mama-and-me juncture painted as something serene and special.

The vision in my head was so saccharine sweet I had all but styled the Hallmark greeting card portrait: Me, all aglow in maternal serenity, flanked by two of the most important people in my world—the woman who had loved and nurtured me, and the little woman-child for whom I would do the same.

But nothing about new motherhood was going as planned. There was no dewy-eyed joy between Mama and me. Mine were the only teary eyes between us. And I hid them—sneaking to the bathroom after Mama's well-intended scoldings. Weeks after giving birth, I felt like mush—literally and figuratively. Vaginal walls were still bleeding and sore. Brain cells, if not dead, were on life support. My once-strong frame felt doughy and fragile. The body that had easily boxed a few rounds in the gym a month prior was now winded walking up the block. The baby was beautiful (in a bug-eyed guppy kind of way). Despite her scrawny looks at five pounds and change, she was healthy. And I loved her with a force that was so strong I could feel the earth shifting around me.

On the flip side, this deep love and all that came with it had rocked my world emotionally. I was both overjoyed and overwrought. One minute I was intoxicatingly happy just looking at my baby. The next, I felt like she was holding me prisoner and I wanted nothing more than for her to get up off me. Moments later, her quiet would awaken me from a sound slumber. Is she breathing? Did she die in her sleep? Then, once up, I'd spend the next several hours racked with guilt over my selfish nonmaternal thoughts. I didn't deserve my baby; I was uncaring, unfit, and unhinged. Just a hot mess.

If I hadn't known better, I might've thought I was suffering some form of postpartum depression. Maybe. No one I knew had ever talked about it directly. There were magazine articles about it that I skimmed over. I had a few of the signs, I thought. But then I'd catch myself, quickly come to my senses—uh-uh, not me. Just saying the word *depression* brought on anxiety. Mama, like many of her generation, had always dismissed that kind of psychobabble. I mean, everyone knows that black women don't have *time* to be depressed. We are far too busy, too practical, too strong, and too—I don't know, too black, I suppose, for that nonsense. When you're a strong black woman you don't sit in quiet reflection or take to your bed in despair like some pinafore-wearing soap opera character. You get up e'ry day—like the old folks say, put one foot in front of the other and keep on keeping on. In other words, you did like Mama.

I could pull things together, I told myself. I just had to snap out of it. I could be strong—just like Mama. Her near-constant admonishments were annoying, but nothing I couldn't deal with. As long as I reminded myself as often as possible that Mama meant well, that it was just her way, I could get through another day of stinging criticism.

I tried to fall back on some of Mama's timeworn axioms. She had several for every conceivable eventuality: *Straighten up and fly right. Act like you know. Check yourself.* The ones that echoed in my head over and over were two she told me in high school: "Much of what you face in life, you face alone. You need to be your own best friend."

If nothing else, Mama was a pragmatist—however brutal. I'd always known that her advice came from years of hardscrabble experience. And while I didn't take it lightly, I never really imagined that any of her cautionary words would apply to my own life. It's not like I was relegated to the back of the bus, couldn't eat at a lunch counter, or had cause to sing the blues on account of a low-down, philandering husband putting his hands on me.

Funny that I now found myself steeled by years of her dark counsel. It seemed ironic, though, that her warnings were not protecting me from the cruelties of the outside world. They were, instead, shielding me from unsympathetic vagaries within the safest love I'd known.

The new dynamic of our relationship was upsetting. But more than that, it was confusing. I was totally undone and totally alone. But it was not all Mama's doing. Left and right, my relationships had begun to careen onto strange—and strained—new paths. My husband, always sweetly detached, was now simply detached—totally oblivious to my gut-churning angst. Usually at all-alone times such as these, I'd turn to my older sister. She didn't have children, but we never needed like circumstances to relate to one another. Unfortunately, she was preoccupied with life crises of her own: a difficult separation from her husband and childhood sweetheart, and problems with Mama (surprise!). I couldn't burden her with a bunch of nagging slights and annoyances that I could barely put a name to.

I did have one good Brooklyn gal pal with whom I'd shared parallel lives for nearly a decade. We were gym buddies in our single days. We were in serious relationships and married at around the same time, and got pregnant at around the same time. She gave birth three months—to the day—before me. I just knew we'd have the kind of bond Mama had with my "other mothers" back home. Our relationship wasn't perfect. Still, it had all the makings of authenticity and promise.

But somewhere during that summer of our nascent motherhood, girlfriend cold flipped. She went from her regular round-the-way self to some kind of freakishly fake automaton mom. Things became a bit suspicious when she brought her baby home. Every time we spoke, she'd tell me things were "Faaabulous!" like we were talking about a new pair of designer shoes she'd just scored at Loehmann's.

Then I would see her around the neighborhood, at times when she didn't see me. And guess what? Things were not looking "Faaabulous!" In fact, she looked tore up, like I'd never seen her before—wearing stretched-out sweats and no makeup. Mind you, this was a sister who'd rocked stiletto heels 24/7 back in the day, tipping along city sidewalks and grates with ease. I totally understood that she was not herself. What I didn't understand was why she felt the need to lie about it. This is how our conversations went:

ME: Hey, girl! Whassup?
HER: *Oooooh, I just loooove being a mom!*
ME: Um . . . Okay . . . So, like, whassup?
HER: *You so crazy. Don't you just loooove being a mom?*
ME: Um . . . You know what? Let me let you go!

Like a bad debt, I had to write her off. Actually, I think she wrote me off. Yeah, she did—started arranging playdates with everybody in the neighborhood except me. Whatever. I was not a total loser. I did have a few true-blue, ace boons. But my closest friends, spread across the country, got married in their twenties and now had school-aged children. If they had any sense of what I was going through, they didn't let on. And I couldn't relate to the mommy groups and new moms I met on the playground who yammered incessantly about all things baby: poop consistency, milestones, sleeping tricks, and the like.

I was a mess back then—so much so that it never occurred to me that Mama was a bit of a mess herself. She'd lost her own mother when she was just a toddler. Mama's new-mom stage had to have been much worse than what I was experiencing. She had no one at all guiding her. Even when Mama was her most meddlesome, most aggravating, most haranguing self, there was no one I would rather have in my corner. And it couldn't have been easy for her to watch me, her baby, caring for my own baby.

For long stretches during the day, Chloe slept "like a truck driver putting in OT," as Mama liked to say. Nice, in a way . . . but it meant lots of idle time. If there's anything that Mama cannot sit still for, it's sitting still. Since retiring from her factory job years earlier, she had begun taking on all manner of work—mixing part-time paying gigs with volunteering. She was a paid companion to several elderly folks in and around town. She drove her church members here and there. And she'd assumed the role of resident Florence Nightingale to the sick and infirm on her block. During her stay, when friends and family called, I overheard Mama waxing proud over how great Chloe was at sleeping ("like a champ," she told them)—something I hadn't recognized as a skill worthy of praise. When no one was calling, Mama was watching *The View* or cleaning my apartment floors on her hands and knees. That got old for her after a while. I suppose she was growing restless.

For sure, I do not know what babies did back in her day. I stayed confused as she vacillated between the two generations' similarities ("Babies need water; I don't care what your doctor says") and their vast differences ("These babies today are so alert and smart; I've never seen anything like it"). But, at any rate, Mama had come prepared to work. It is what she did best. In hindsight, my breast-feeding plan probably knocked several chores off her intended to-do list. There was no bottle heating, scrubbing, sterilizing, or soaking—which I imagine could keep one busy for hours. Within a few days, Mama announced that she was leaving to go back home, much to my protests. "You guys have everything under control," she insisted.

Nothing was under control, as far as I could tell. Yes, the baby did seem to sleep pretty well. But she didn't sleep *all* the time. In fact, at night when Mama was getting her z's, Chloe was wide awake. And in my naïveté, I assumed that through her whimpering and squirming she was trying to tell me something. Maybe she was hungry. Maybe she was too hot or too cold. Maybe her diaper needed changing. And, Lord Jesus, when Chloe needed changing in those first few nights, all hell would break loose.

She would let out this piercing wail like she was the Exorcist Girl when the wet diaper came off. And the decibel levels soared off the charts once the baby wipes reached her nickel-sized butt. If that weren't scary enough, the child's whole body—which, I remind you, was about the size of a large rodent—would tremble and shake.

Come morning, I would try to retell the horror story of predawn events to Mama. But I could never manage to convince her of how awful the fright-night experience had been. She would usually blow me off, laughing, and remind me of how "dramatic" I tend to be.

I know that she hadn't meant to be hurtful. But she also had a habit of running off a long list of things I should've done to avoid Chloe's meltdown. Tops on the list was proper swaddling. "Did you wrap her like I showed you?" she'd ask. "Did you pat her butt?" "Did you rub her back?" To me, it was as though she were saying: "What did *you* do to make the baby go all Linda Blair? She's an angel with me."

I tried to convince Mama that my obvious shortcomings were all the more reason for her to stay with me a while longer. No such luck.

Within a couple of days, she was on the phone with my sister talking flight times, change fees, and area airports. I started to get up and make one more appeal as they confirmed the details. But I could barely move—let alone get out of bed. I had body aches, fever, and chills. I was weak in a bone-tired kind of way, exceedingly more intense than the normal new-mom state of sleep deprivation. When I tried to sit up in bed, I had to fight against the weight of two strange new breasts—Wendy Williams–sized mammaries that sat swollen, hot, and throbbing on my chest. They were rock hard, like a Hollywood boob job gone wrong. And, did I mention that they were freakishly large? My breasts had become engorged, bordering mastitis, a dangerous infection caused by plugged milk ducts. My precious, innocent baby—the one who slept like a champ—had jacked me up.

Mama was, understandably, worried and—perhaps—more convinced than ever that this nursing business was plain old foolishness to the nth degree. I suppose I did look kind of crazy, with one hand holding compresses to the mountainous "breastesses" hovering near chin level and the other hand trying to cradle the phone as hotline experts from the lactation gurus of La Leche League talked me through recovery steps. Within the next forty-eight hours my fever had subsided and my swollen boobies had begun to look more *Real Housewives* and a bit less stripperlike. Mama was relieved—as was I—and set her relatively guilt-free departure in motion. Although I didn't know exactly what to expect in this early stage of motherhood, I was thoroughly certain that Mama was leaving me in the lurch just as projectile poop was likely to hit the fan.

In a show of vulnerability I had certainly not been raised with, I asked Mama over and over to stay awhile longer. I did not hint or beat around the bush. I said words like, *"I need you."* Repeatedly I said, "Don't go." During the last few weeks of my pregnancy we'd agreed she'd stay for two weeks. Now, she was itching to get back to Buffalo. Her dog needed her. Mrs. So-and-So in the hospital had been calling. Her grass was overgrown. To hear her talk, it was almost as though nothing and no one in Buffalo could get by without her. She was needed by everyone she could think of—except me. This one had bursitis. That one needed someone to drive her to the grocery store. Me, on the other hand? Mama had decided her work here was done. For all I knew, my breastesses could again become infected. And, while I'm not one to squabble, there was very little food in my fridge. There was a grocery store within walking distance, as she well knew from previous visits. What was a sister-girl supposed to do for dinner? I saw plenty of useful things she could've been doing to keep busy.

Yet, a heartbeat after her own baby (I am the youngest, after all) had ejected a human being—her only grandbaby—in my mother's estimation I was "going to be just fine."

In hindsight Mama was growing increasingly uneasy

with each passing day. Although Mama didn't really "do" feelings very well, she undoubtedly had a complex web of emotions stirring inside her. That became startlingly clear one evening when the baby was lying quietly in her bassinet as Mama and I cleaned up the kitchen after dinner. My husband was working late and the house was still, save for the music wafting through our Brooklyn apartment. The last cut from *The Miseducation of Lauryn Hill* was winding to a close. It was followed in the queue by what I thought was some random collection of old black spirituals called "In the Hollow of Your Hand." To save my life, I cannot remember how I came to own it. I was working at a magazine at the time, so most likely it was a promotional disc. I'm not even sure when I got it. The CD wasn't in regular rotation, but since bringing the baby home I'd begun playing it more often. On this night, as always, the gentle hymns were like a soothing embrace after a stress-filled day.

I assumed they were spirituals. But, truth be told, I hadn't the slightest idea. I'd been meaning to read the liner notes, but with the baby and all I simply hadn't gotten around to actually doing it. None of these mysteries stopped me from enjoying the sound. The rhythms were deep and almost haunting—in a good way. There was achingly beautiful guitar strumming accompanied by lyrics I never even tried to make out—an indecipherable combination of the sort of slave dialect you read past in historical fiction, a lot of "I'se a-goin'" and "dese li'l babies." Together the words and melody were so rich and moving, I didn't need to know exactly what the song was about.

As the tunes played—one more poignant and woeful than the first—I could swear I heard the sound of muffled cries in the distance. Reflexively, my attention immediately went toward the bassinet in the living room, even though the sounds were nothing like the whines of an infant.

"Mama?" I whispered. This was scary. I'd heard my mother cry on exactly one occasion in my life: when Papa died Christmas night more than thirty years ago. She wasn't the sniveling kind. "You okay?"

"It's Grandma Josie," she stammered, composing herself. "She used to sing this lullaby to me after my mother passed away . . ."

CHAPTER THREE

Don't Start Smelling Yourself

It may not appear that we'd have much in common. But across the subway car, girlfriend and I locked eyes in that kind of split-second moment of recognition when soul-to-soul stuff happens. I don't know what it is exactly. But it is as though our hearts cross and the ancestors start spilling tea. It feels like the Sledge chicks sang in the seventies: "I got all my sisters with me." It's a black thing that sometimes even I don't understand. But it's for real. There's me, dressed in Gap capris and ballet flats—channeling Audrey Hepburn from back in the day. Then there's girlfriend, rocking Timberlands, Apple Bottom jeans, and dookie braids from around the way. We'd barely made eye contact until we both heard the screams coming from a stroller in the middle aisle on a crowded train. At first, it was difficult to figure out what was bothering the child— all the yelling, the writhing, the squirming—but he seemed determined to escape the stroller harness. He was off the rails in the throes of toddler-tantrum speak . . . red-faced and buck wild. Then he threw his sippy cup at his mother's pregnant belly and wailed, "I *HATE* you!" Despite the no-drip claims, said sippy cup did in fact leak. And as the kid's mom dabbed her damp blond bangs, she simply sighed and said, "We're almost home, Billy . . . There, there."

I looked up at girlfriend just as girlfriend looked at me. Our faces high-fived each other across the crowded train and our eyes spoke. Hers said, "Oh, *HELL* no he didn't." And mine responded: "Yes. He. Did." Then girlfriend started to shake her head slowly and smile. I laughed. And we reveled in our bonding time. It's that moment when black women share a secret without uttering a word. Not everyone knows we have secrets. Our confidences are not perceptible to outsiders, because that's just how we roll. We keep secrets from men. We keep secrets from white people. We keep secrets from our secrets. Yes. It's that deep. And it's why we love one another with a fierceness no words can describe. That shared knowingness is the number-one reason that Michelle Obama is our shero. The connection is so powerful I can only begin to explain by borrowing the words of the rapper who famously hails from Marcy Projects ("H" to the "O.V."): "Real recognize real . . . and you're looking familiar."

Have you ever looked—I mean really looked—at that sister's face? Obviously, it is saying: *I am the First Lady of the United States of America.* You quickly perceive her intelligence, grace, and beauty. But what she communicates to us black women is homegirl through and through. Birthers question her man's citizenship. Feminists assail her at-home mothering choice. But while she is standing on a podium smiling and looking classy as all get-out to the rest of the known world, the glint in her eyes is telling us: *Haters gon' hate. You know how we do!*

I know it's easy to get the impression from all the neck-rolling Sapphire-ness on TV that we black women holler and fuss all day long—that we loud-talk folks, read them for every little transgression. But in the quiet beneath the noise, I would wager that we are probably the most discreet, still, and discerning population on the face of the earth. And we keep many, many things on the low. Especially when it comes to motherhood.

Allow me to explain. I'll begin with a bit of a qualifier. You know when the gossip starts to get really good and a friend begins a statement with, "I don't want to sound mean, but . . ." Inevitably, the words that follow will be spiteful and cruel. Right? The same is true when someone says, "Not to sound racist, but . . ."

There is no shame in my game. I won't preface what I'm about to say with any attempt to be politically correct, because the words I'm about to say are, well, you know . . . racist. I will own it. No mistake. Racial stereotypes are, of course, built on racist assumptions.

But, in all fairness, you know sometimes when people spout racial stereotypes, they can be a-little-bit-kinda true. Not entirely true, but a smidgen. For example, as a black person myself, I have never met another black person who did not like chicken. I know some vegans who don't *eat* chicken. But that's different. I never met one who didn't *like* chicken. On the other hand, we don't all eat watermelon. My son, Cole, can't stand watermelon and I know others who are not fond of it—admittedly, not very many.

Not all black people can dance either. Mama couldn't find a beat if it were pounded upside her head. In stark contrast to the venerable "Skeleton Song," I have long harbored serious doubt that Mama's hip bone is in fact connected to (or within a half-mile radius of) her backbone. She doesn't even have a little bit of rhythm. And I went to college with a sister whose dancing was so bad she thought she was good. In fact, her Greek pledge name was "Crazy Legs," and it was emblazoned on her sorority jacket. That her so-called sisters would play her in such a way was all the confirmation I ever needed to remain Me Phi Me. It was freshman year, I think, and Kool and the Gang had a song out called "Fresh." I tell you, that poor girl would rush the dance floor in a fitful frenzy, her bony limbs going every which way. It was sad, really. But I digress.

Just as mainstream America has promulgated certain stereotypes about blacks, we have done the same. There is one particular stereotype I'd always heard, one that never completely resonated until I became a mom. It truly pains me to say it, but I think it's better that you all hear it from me—not in the streets. So here goes:

White parents are punks.

Aahhh. It feels good to finally let that out. I've never really put it out there before. Generally speaking, every black person on the face of the earth believes this to be gospel. Yes. We hold this truth to be self-evident . . . That white kids are born with a license to run all over their parents, especially their mothers—with the only repercussion being a tap of the foot and some lame response like, "Now, Becky . . ."

The belief is so pervasive that when two black people—who are TOTAL strangers and wouldn't otherwise give each other the time of day—observe a white toddler falling out in a public place, they instinctively connect and nod in agreement. Sometimes they trade nonverbal cues like head shaking or eye rolling. They might even laugh. Same thing happens when a white teenager is overheard screaming, "Mom, shut up!" or "What's the friggin' big deal?" Here is what black people don't say out loud, but think:

- "Is anyone else seeing and hearing what I'm seeing and hearing?"
- "Where is my belt? I'm gon' beat this child's behind. Then Imma whip his fool mama!"
- "White folks . . . go figure."

Before you go and get yourself all offended, I hope you realize I'm sharing this information only out of love. The way I figure, if we want to know the crazy thoughts whites have about black people, all we have to do is watch Fox News. But you poor white people have no way to get the 411. If you tried watching BET, you've probably already been led astray, because, honestly, not that many black folks have as much sex as the average hip-hop star. Especially married folks. I know one thing: Even if "I been drankin'," we don't hardly be "all night."

Make no mistake. Disclosures like this are risky business for a sister and could possibly cost me my black card. This may come as a surprise to many of you, but there are certain things black people are not supposed to do or say in mixed company. I'm not making this up. It's a hard-and-fast rule—a regulation . . . subject to very harsh judgment and shame.

Think about it. When conservative blacks talk openly about the state of black families and other recent trends in our culture there is always an uproar in inner-city barbershops and beauty parlors across the country. Why are people really upset? Not always because the observations are off base. Who among "us" have not been frustrated at times by the behavior of other black and brown folks? Who among "us" have not been stumped in crooked-eye wonder by the upsurge in names like Taliqua and JaQuan? (By the way, if you have been so named, I've got love for you. I'm just saying, "Why?," that's all.) Black folks are mostly upset by how and where such things are said: in front of y'all. Out loud. With cameras rolling.

In fairness, to both whites and blacks, we get most of our opinions on one another from what we see on television. Black moms on TV—probably from the first famous one, Julia, to Clair Huxtable—were on their grind. Carol Brady had Alice around all the time, although I can't recall her holding down a gig. And even though Weezy Jefferson had Florence, the show's dialogue suggested that she had helped George build up the dry-cleaning business. I'm not defending my ignorance. I'm just saying. Alas. Why can't we all just be like Barack and try to create a "more perfect union"? I think at this point we should be open and honest about our prejudices and backward thinking. Own it. [Note to black folks: Fall back; I'm not planning to spill everything.]

It's a scientific and well-researched fact that blacks and whites operate under a different set of expectations—a different set of goals—when it comes to parenting. Many black parents believe that obedience and respect for elders are the main measures of a kid raised right—which explains why you're more likely to see a black child get yoked in public if he acts out. I don't think most white parents place as high a premium on compliance (duh?). Instead, they rank things like confidence and autonomy high on the scale of "good kids."

Confidence, in the black households I know, is generally not to be openly displayed by kids. Be black and proud and all that good stuff outside the house. But under Mom and Dad's roof, children are not encouraged to act like they're all that. It's a black thing. And I know it sounds a bit confusing. Even as I'm talking, I'm beginning to question the logic of it. But that's just the thing. The issue is not so much about logic as it is history.

Here's a teeny picture: Both my parents were born and raised down South—Mama in Birmingham, and Dad in a three-square-mile patch of South Carolina, near Spartanburg, called Pacolet.

Although they separated when I was about five years old, in some ways, we lived like an intact family—spending untold outings, holidays, and vacations together. Go figure.

One summer we all piled into Dad's faux wood–paneled station wagon to travel to a family reunion in St. Louis. We were very excited to see arches that dwarfed McDonald's. But for Mama the trip was very special. This St. Louis crew, which had migrated from Mississippi, was the only connection she had to her own mother—who died when she was just a toddler. It seemed to me that her mom's brother, Uncle Fineness—I swear I'm not making that name up—was her favorite. Rather than return home to Buffalo with our parents, apparently the grown-ups decided that I and my older brother and sister should spend the rest of our summer vacation in Mississippi, our maternal grandmother's birthplace. Some kind of *Roots* experiment, I suppose.

Us kids weren't especially keen on the trip. But our newly discovered cousins talked it up like it was Disneyland— bragging that they had an in-ground pool and all kinds of luxuries. When we first set foot in Mississippi—Macon, to be exact, a city of about three thousand people in the northeastern part of the state—I quickly surmised that the "pool" talk had been a figment of somebody's overactive imagination. "Rainy," "Brisco," "Bunt": one of my cousins must've thought the watering hole—murky, muddy, with flies swarming—was *like* a pool. Or maybe it was their idea of a joke. From the looks of Macon's endless cornfields and dirt roads, my adventuresome six-year-old brain convinced the rest of me that this trip would be very exciting— like a real-life version of *The Beverly Hillbillies.*

Things didn't quite go down like that, though. We did have fun. My aunt Annie Bell had cows and pigs—very cool until the novelty wore off and the stench set in. I adored all my cousins. Never mind that it took a long time to understand what they were saying—especially Shad, so cool and full of charm I figured he'd gotten his name from that Sly Stone "Loose Booty" song (remember the chanting, "Shadrach, Meshach, Abednego"?). But something just wasn't right. It was the 1970s and even as a child I could almost smell the racial tension, although I wasn't completely familiar with the scent. When my uncle Sol took us to town—where there were actual sidewalks and stores, not just dirt and farmland—it was the highlight of our visit. Aunt Annie Bell had us kids get all dressed up, sort of. And I think she put on a nice hat. She'd been talking it up all week—so much that in my head we were going someplace really fancy.

But once we got there, hot and wrinkled from the drive, Auntie did not seem so chipper. She always smiled. But on this trip only her mouth was smiling, not her eyes. And she was talking to us in a soft tone of voice, like the downtown streets of Columbus were a library or something. My uncle Sol, so naturally good and pleasant he could've passed himself off as Mr. Rogers's black understudy, had turned almost somber, it seemed to me, despite the corners of his lips being slightly upturned.

There were white people *everywhere* and seeing them downtown like that served to remind me that I had seen few white faces during our stay. As the white people walked along, I noticed that my uncle kept stepping to the side—walking nearly in the street at times. The whites never said, "Excuse me." They never asked him to move, but move he did. After witnessing this a few times, I noticed that the white people were not so much walking along the sidewalk. They were charging through like they owned the whole town. Come to think of it, had Uncle Sol not moved they might've mowed him down. It was as though on a narrow road they were Mack trucks and my uncle was a Ford Pinto. Not only did he allow them the right of way, he tipped his hat—over and over again to the white passersby. I knew his head had to be tired from all that nodding and tipping, like a bobblehead doll. That wasn't all; Uncle would then bare his teeth, forming something that passed for a smile, and say, "How do, sir, how do?" to each and every one of them. I took notice that his greetings were met with stony silence. None of the white people even looked in his direction, in fact.

It was all very jarring to me. My older brother and sister were more than unsettled. They were fired up. I mean pissed to the highest level of pissivity. Bordering on sass, they kept asking, "Why are you speaking to all these people? They sure don't seem like your friends." Auntie kept trying to hush them and Uncle Sol just shook his head— sort of half smiling. He didn't like all their questions any more than Aunt Annie Bell did. But it wasn't his nature to be cross or fuss.

When we got back from our Down South adventure and shared some of the stories, my parents laughed. They were more amused by our indignation than the retelling of events, which apparently were not the least bit surprising or newsworthy for them. My father laughed loudest (no surprise). Whether he was the giver or receiver of the story, nobody enjoyed a tale more than he. Even if he had to make it up whole cloth, Dad was going to find the funny in any and every circumstance. He howled, "Ohhh, Lord! You kids are lucky whitey didn't call the *Po-Po*. Down there you can't act all high and mighty like that around white folks. . . . Mess around and get shot!

"I remember one time . . ." Mama, of course, cut him off with a stern look that said, *Shut the hell up.* She sometimes used her words, but just like with us kids, Mama had a stony grill that far exceeded the limits of verbal articulation. My dad quickly obliged. He didn't like static. When

Mama shot that *don't start none; won't be none* look, she shut things down. He was certainly no saint, but you couldn't help but feel bad during these times. If Dad didn't have real love for Mama, he was relentless in offering up his own counterfeit brand. Mama, trained to put the *diss* in *dysfunction*, routinely met his exuberant affectations with eye-rolling frustration.

In that particular moment, I wanted to hear one of his stories. I was still a bit confused by what I'd seen in Mississippi. Maybe I was secretly hoping that with Dad's boisterous spin on the situation it would be a little less unsettling. Up until that point, all I'd known of black-white relations was "cracker this" and "honky that"—more or less Flip Wilson style. It never dawned on me that white people were to be feared. I'd seen Black Panthers on television—they were badass brothers and sisters all.

It was years before I understood a fraction of what my parents lived through down South. Blacks from their generation, and generations prior, knew "high and mighty" talk came at a price. That's why mouthing off—to this day—is not to be taken lightly in a black family. Obedience is next to godliness. Curiosity, acting out, or any uppity or seemingly ill-mannered behavior simply can't be tolerated.

Of course, I've never heard Mama or any black mother actually *say* that too much confidence is a bad thing. But it was implicit in even the most mundane parenting interactions. What happens is this: A kid reaches a certain stage—not so much an age, mind you—wherein a sense of supreme confidence begins to well up inside. Said child becomes aware of her power, starts to feel emboldened; ask questions; challenge authority. This is a good thing. Right? Well, now that all depends. In theory the emergence of self-esteem is something we parents all want to see in our children.

But there is also a huge downside once you began asserting yourself in too bold a fashion. And Mama would let you know she wasn't having it. She was quick to say: *"Don't start smelling yourself up in here!"* (Translation: Don't get too big for your britches.)

Do not despair, white moms and dads. I have seen for myself that many of you are not at all punks. You are, to be sure, far more, um, flexible, than most black parents. We simply have different expectations and discipline styles. Here is just a brief sampling of things Mama would say that I don't believe a white person would *ever* say to their child.

- "I'll slap the taste outcha mouth!"
- "If you want to keep your eyeballs in your head, you bet' not roll them again."
- "You don't have to run away; you can walk. And I won't chase after you."

- "Don't let your mouth write a check that your ass can't cash."

Just because roughly four million black people claim something to be true doesn't make it so. We blacks have been off the mark with our stereotyping in the past. Once upon a time, for example, it was widely theorized that all white girls had flat booties. Period.

It wasn't unusual to speak ill of a white girl back in the day by saying something like, "That no-ass Suzy had the nerve . . ." My, how times have changed. Most blacks have shed such prejudices, as a lot of white girls now pack serious junk in their trunks. In fact, per Anna Wintour— so thin her backside could stunt double for her front and doyenne of all things current and culturally relevant—2014 officially marked the Era of the Big Booty. Not because of sisters whose behinds have crossed zip codes for generations. Not because Sir Mix-a-Lot waxed poetic some twenty years ago when he spit "Baby Got Back." No. The Booty Era is here because of big-ass wannabes like Iggy Azalea and the Kardashians. *Vogue* could've dug deeper and found white girls with real, not silicone-enhanced, big butts. I've seen them. In fact, as a race, blacks have taken notice. Instead of unfounded generalizations, our opinions are now shaped by sound scientific factors, including the interrace marriage rates and contemporary white America's Columbusing of all things black—like hip-hop, cornrows, and, of course, chicken (fried, I suspect).

Don't shoot the messenger, people. Think of the information I'm dropping in these pages as one thick and, at times, rambling public service announcement. Remember that trench coat–wearing TV hound dog warning us as kids to "Take a bite out of crime"? He talked about some scary stuff and probably made us anxious, but we needed to know about nefarious characters that might try to snatch up blond, blue-eyed girls like Amy. Notice how McGruff never cautioned that anybody might grab Sheneika or deal drugs to Daiquan? If you missed that nuance, don't think it got past us black people. The message we get pretty much all the time is that white children are worthy of being protected. They are precious.

I'm not saying that many whites consciously think this way nowadays. But the relationship between white kids and black women as their protectors and caregivers goes way back. Ever since "Plymouth Rock landed on us," as Malcolm X said, black women have been caregivers to white children, often even nursing them on plantations. These black women usually had children of their own (sold from under them), as do many of the black nannies pushing white children in strollers today.

Black people love their kids, for sure. But historically we never had the luxury of thinking them precious. Special? Yes. There is a big difference. We don't see our kids as anything akin to fine china, not to be disturbed or broken. In fact, given our druthers, most black parents would choose to "break" their kids before someone else does. So habits like speaking out of turn, acting out in public, or any action that draws the scrutiny of outsiders is to be halted—immediately. We fear that if we wait for our kids to simply outgrow such childishness, they might suffer at the hands of authority, especially those men in blue. Authority, with its billy sticks and handcuffs and black robes, has not been kind to us. Too much adoring, too much lovey-dovey cooing might fill a child's head with thoughts that would get him killed. Surely the overseer, the Klansman, the beat cop—or whoever—might find that confident black kid arrogant and do him harm.

Mama almost never talks about the past—especially the messy parts. I once read that Martin Luther King Jr. said that Birmingham, her birthplace, was to desegregation what Johannesburg was to apartheid. When I asked Mama about that statement, she would only say, "You know good and well I've never been to South Africa."

CHAPTER FOUR

Check Yourself before You Wreck Yourself

I have secrets. Deep. Dark. Secrets. The kind of secrets that would make you alter your opinion of me. I've done things—things of which I am not proud. Sick things, really. I won't make excuses. I have no one to blame but myself. Mama didn't raise me to act a fool.

See, what had happened was . . . *Scratch that*. I don't really know what happened.

All I can say now is that I'm sorry. I'm sorry I brought shame to my family. I'm sorry for setting back the sisterhood of women. I'm sorry I let down my race. I guess I just lost my way. Maybe something snapped. But I know if I stand any chance for redemption, I know I have to admit my wrongs. . . . Here goes.

- I used to peel the skin off peas to make them easier for my babies to digest. Each and every pea. With writer's carpal-tunneled fingers. Each casing meticulously removed. Oh, and of course, the peas had to be organic. (It never dawned on me that as a nursing mom, the pesticide-infested foods *I* was grubbing could kill them just as well.)

- Pedestrian products like Johnson's baby lotion were not good enough for *my* babies. Long before news broke that cancer-causing chemicals like phthalates—which I can't even pronounce—were rampant in common drugstore brands, I'd become a connoisseur of expensive specialty diaper creams and potions.

- I once considered using a baby wipe warmer. I received it as a shower gift. After a few minutes' reconsidering, I did decide against it. But in the spirit of atonement, I want to come clean—totally.

- From infancy to around age four, I planned my entire day around my kids' sleep times—come hell or high water their heads had to hit the mattress by one P.M. Car and stroller naps were out of the question. A rigid bath-book-bed chain of events was a near-sacred ritual never to be broken, amended, or in any way dishonored.

- Having some vague recollection of a Beech-Nut baby food recall in the early 1990s, I decided my kids would not ingest any Beech-Nut or Gerber (just to be on the safe side) products ever in life.

- I composed and printed out long, detailed itineraries of when my kids should eat, sleep, and play—to the minute (for example, *9:15–10:00: "free play" time*)—for any and all caregivers. I saved the document on my PC and updated it every few weeks or so, as the baby grew and changed. Needless to say, when I presented said rundown to Mama, a flurry of cussing ensued.

So there we have it. I was a hot mess. There is lots more to this line of foolishness. It was a multilayered mess—not just a thin coating. But you get the picture. On the outside, I didn't *look* crazy. I would typically front like I was all laid-back and carefree. But inside was a different story. I was like a functioning alcoholic; all but those closest to me thought I had it going on. And I told myself the same. The reality is I wasn't being authentic . . . wasn't living my truth. I know that now because Oprah told me so. Well, she didn't tell me directly. But you know what I mean.

Here's the thing. Having kids scared the living daylights out of me. I mostly enjoyed being pregnant. I liked buying the stuff that went along with having kids. And since mine were easily the most beautiful creatures God ever blew life into, I loved holding my kids, dressing my kids, and carrying them around. I've never been a hot celebrity. I don't know what it feels like to have paparazzi following my every move. But let's be honest, when you walk around with a baby—and, again, not to belabor the point, but my babies were blessed with epic cuteness and uber charm . . . to the point where I feel compelled to offer up my deepest apologies to average babies (of which, sadly, there are many)—these babies are like achieving instant rock star status.

New moms are suddenly catapulted into this realm of irrefutable significance. There are news reports, studies, and all manner of important cultural discussions that revolve totally around you. And look around. Would Tide and Motrin and all these multinational billion-dollar corporations be paying this much attention to you if you were not inherently valuable? I mean, not to throw this in anybody's face, but I took an economics class at Northwestern with a nationally renowned Keynesian expert. Full disclosure: I still don't understand the whole guns-and-butter thing, and Professor Eisner generously gave me a D in the class. But the point is, if an entire industry sprouts up largely based on the workings of *my* vajayjay, I am important. Okay? And you can't tell me nothing!

Now putting aside the macroeconomic piece—or maybe it's micro (as noted, I got a D)—consider what happens within a mom's unit of family and friends. Everybody wants to stop by. People bring gifts. They want to see pictures. You acquire a bunch of cute nicknames. If you are not black or Latina, probably no one has ever referred to you as Li'l Mama or Mami. And if you *are* black or Latina, the tag resonates now more than ever. The folks who have known you your whole life look at you differently now. Literally. I mean they start dissecting the shape of your eyes, the corners of your mouth, and the slope of your nostrils. The burning issue from the moment you pop out a tiny creature is, of course, whom does it take after? Which parent has the dominant DNA? Which features came from whom? Friends and family get all up in your grill to settle the point.

Like much of celebrity life, some of this attention gets annoying. And most moms will put up "Kardashian-like" complaints: on the one hand grumbling about folks' laser-focused preoccupation, then the next minute plastering selfies or baby pictures—which are kind of the same thing—all over social media. Personally, I can say that I would be nothing without my fans—er, I mean, my friends and family. For example, how on earth did I manage to go through life, prebaby, without the critical self-awareness that I was born with hanging, not attached, earlobes? In the name of all that is good and holy, all I can say is, "Thank God for motherhood."

One more thing—and this is big. Before I birthed his children, my husband, Mark, liked me quite a bit. Even loved me, he'd say. I got on his nerves some, naturally. But he thought I was a nice wife. He regarded me as competent and book smart. I was no ingénue when we got married. I'd lived on my own for several years, maintained an apartment; I had good credit and such. But I don't think I was particularly special in his eyes. You can't tell him we talked about this. He would only deny it. But I think he thought *he* was the strong one in our coupling—the real brains of the operation. When we went to the gym, he completed his workout with military-style focus. On the other hand, if I bumped into an old friend, my treadmill run slowed to a snail's pace while I yammered on for thirty minutes. And don't let my music skip or die. My "workout" ground to a halt. He never understood how my entire fitness plan could rest on a Busta Rhymes track. Surely, if I needed M.O.P., Remy Ma, and Bussa Buss to hold my hand through squats and push-ups, I was not very strong of mind or purpose.

Then there was the whole money management thing. See, the first month we were married, living in an alleged one-bedroom apartment in the West Village, I mailed the rent check—but forgot to sign it. The landlord was not pressed. These things happen. Right? Well, Mark made up his mind that he needed to be in charge of household finances. I don't think he intentionally downgraded my worth. In fact, in hindsight, I think like most of us do in relationships he created a narrative that best suited him—

and his own self-image. He was the one who knew more, could do more, could handle more. He was serious and exceedingly capable. I was a bit of a flake—cute and well-meaning, but a flake nonetheless. With childbirth, all that changed.

I'd made him proud—perhaps, for the very first time. I'd produced something, achieved something, great. Despite my frivolity. Despite my inadequate sports knowledge, technical aptitude, and emotional neediness. Mark saw me as strong and powerful, if not inimitable. It was sweet. But I failed to appreciate the lovey-dovey mush. I let my new-found power go to my head. There was no humility. I was like, "*Yeeaaaah*, baby! Check out Mother Earth over here, y'all!"

Three words danced in my head: "YOU BETTER RECOGNIZE!"

I got lost in the sauce. And without even thinking, I threw my superiority in Mark's face. The baby needed this, not that. No matter what he thought, I knew better. The baby was not hungry, she was sleepy. I, and only I, knew when she was gassy. In fact, I could anticipate her every need. After all, I was the mother. I now had skills few could ever possess. I had intuition—which meant I had this direct line of communication to the source of omnipotent wisdom. So there. *How ya like me now?*

While I was getting drunk off my kind-of-a-big-deal

status and channeling my inner Kanye West, I think I knew something was amiss. I was not at all like myself. Being a celebrity is very, very hard work, you see. That's probably why you always hear stories of celebrities' outrageous demands. The way I see it, if you're Jennifer Lopez or Mariah Carey and your public is constantly swarming, probably you start to feel as though your life is not your own and you develop a need to control the little things. You know the stories of stars' demands: bowls full of M&Ms with the green ones removed, vases of white lilies, Evian water to bathe in. That was me, sort of—with the peeling peas and lists of do's and don'ts. I fancy myself a lot like JLo and Mimi—only I've got a bit of a struggle booty and a pint-sized bank account. Otherwise, we are exactly the same. I had much in common with these bold-faced names. I may have been smiling on the outside. But as a famous hip-hop sage so eloquently put it, "sometimes I'd get the blues so hard you would think I was Crippin'" (true that, Fabolous).

And I wasn't alone. I believe that many women like me, who had children later in life and then adjusted their careers to accommodate their new priorities, were similarly displaced. Motherhood had become not just an act of loving and raising a child but a cultural movement. Were we looking to make child rearing our new profession? Somehow elevate natural maternal instincts to corporate-level status? Or did the media and marketing worlds see us coming and seize an opportunity to sell us on aspirational gimmickry?

I will certainly own my crazy. But women have always been far more susceptible than men to the whole how-to-do-anything-better pitch. The not-the-least-bit-subtle inference is that in and of ourselves we are simply not enough. Not thin enough. Not pretty enough. Not sexy enough. Not assertive enough. Not submissive enough. Why should mothering be any different? A bunch of white guys on Madison Avenue decided to exploit our insecurities to create a market out of motherhood, a process God made as natural as breathing.

The culture was ripe for the picking with all the Dr. Phil-izing on TV and self-help books filling store shelves. Like a lot of women driven by career, I was far, far away from family who could support and ground me. Had I been back in Buffalo, Sugar—Mama's best friend and my godmother—would've simply sat me down and said, "Baby, you need *JESUS!*"

Instead I thought I needed T. Berry Brazelton's *Touchpoints: Birth to Three* and a baby monitor with audio and motion sensors.

At the time, I was simply trying to raise my kid in a more enlightened fashion. I believed that if I kept on top of children's health news and parenting studies and adjusted my habits accordingly, all the effort might help me to be a better parent—which, in turn, meant I would have "better" kids (better than what, I'm not sure). It all began innocently enough.

Don't forget, I am a journalist. And I do like my news—the *New York Times*, the *Wall Street Journal*, the *New York Post*—consuming vast amounts of information had always been my thing. Some people love chocolate and wine. I love Page Six and the Jane Brody column, with a li'l dark chocolate and a glass of Shiraz on the side . . . Don't judge me, okay?

I wasn't hurting anybody. Save for a handful of annoying predilections, I might not have turned into a full-blown nutcase. But then something happened. My career took a sudden turn. I accidentally became a parenting editor. I didn't trip and fall—but it was something like that. I don't think anyone sets out to become one of these oddities. As a little girl, I wasn't lying across my twin bed with thoughts of editing stories like "8 Ways to Tame a Tantrum" and "How to Please Your Picky Eater."

I happened to have written a freelance piece on parenting—specifically, it was what to do if your kid is bullied. Instinctively I placed Mama smack in the middle of my reporting. She'd always told me that if someone raised a hand to me I should make sure I was the last person they *ever* hit. Was I supposed to maim or kill said schoolyard bully? I'm not sure. Like a lot of what Mama said, you just didn't question these things.

Of course, I pointed out that one didn't operate that way in these times. Aside from being immature, such advice was potentially dangerous; JaQuan would surely return to the scene with his cousins and 'em—at least one of whom might be packing. Anyway, it just so happened that the person in charge of that section of the magazine was a particularly trifling sort. And when I handed in my piece, she was off on a trip—leaving her triflingness exposed. My friend, who was editor-in-chief, and the antithesis of trifling behavior, fired her and hired me.

Let's just say, that's when the projectile spit-up hit the fan. My near-obsessive need for up-to-the-minute information became a necessary part of my J-O-B.

Lawd, Jesus! Take the wheel!

CHAPTER FIVE

Let's Take It to the Bridge

Old people like to say certain children "have been here before." It means they are wise beyond their years— old souls. Well, I'm not normally one to boast. But my second-born, had apparently "been here" and back so many times she could write the GPS coordinates. Baby Girl delivered *HERSELF*!

It was around midnight when we arrived at the hospital. My water had broken about an hour prior, in the middle of an *ER* episode. There was no hours-long buildup, like I'd had with Chloe. Labor went from zero to 100. Real. Quick. From the minute I sprung that leak, my body started throbbing. My thighs hurt. My back ached. And my entire pelvis was ablaze with the pressure of a massive gelatinous orb slowly, steadily grinding itself through my crotch. Think mortar and pestle over a Bunsen burner.

After the tortuous act of changing into the booty-peeking gown, I managed to lay my excruciatingly pained lower half on the cot. For a moment I thought I might black out. My sight got blurry and I heard the faint sound of my doctor being paged on the PA system. Other than that, I was in a daze of agonizing proportions. In an attempt to get some modicum of comfort I decided to lie on my right side. During pregnancy, women are always warned to lie ONLY on their left sides, but I guess misery brought out the rebel in me. I was going for that right side—sort of. I mean I was *trying* to. But what with my loins on fire and all, even the slight movement was tricky. For reasons I could not fathom at the time, it was near impossible for me to actually shut my thighs. So with legs spread-eagle and all akimbo, I began to muster small, gingerly movements, ordered just so, to shift my now-sizable body weight—first using my hands, then my elbows. If you are wondering what Mark was doing during this whole Cirque du Soleil experience, you are not alone. But it's actually a good thing he wasn't trying to help me get situated, because somewhere in the middle of the death-defying act of setting my knees upright . . . that pressure ball of a human form I told you about earlier, the one burrowing a large grotto between my legs? Well, she shot out of my flaming womb like a cannon in a twenty-one-gun salute.

If not for Mark and his wide-receiver past, things

would've ended badly—very badly. Daddy caught Baby Girl, right after he leaped straight into the air and let out a shriek—part manly, partly not so much (he denies the sound effects, laying claim only to the winning catch, but I know what I know). Probably we were both shrieking, because the nurses on duty all came running.

I was thoroughly spooked. I mean, sure, every mom wants a speedy delivery. But not freaky-deaky style. I felt like I was in one of those B-movie flicks where the pus-filled alien forms burst out of the bodies of everyday people.

But here's the plot twist. Once the ooze and blood were wiped off, Trinity was about as perfect a baby specimen as I'd ever seen. I mean fresh-out-the-gate gorgeous. She had lots of shiny dark hair, footlong eyelashes, and these elegant little piano-player hands with long tissue-paper-thin fingernails. And at six pounds and change, girlfriend was a decent fighting weight. She looked less like an abandoned sparrow and more like a sweet, fleshy cherub.

And I knew life could not get any better than that moment. To this day, I remember that awestruck feeling of swooning, nose-wide-open love and adoration. Once in a while, Trinity still can make my heart skip a beat. I guess that's why she's my favorite child. But please don't tell anyone, because mothers are really not supposed to say such things.

Her theatrical entrance into the world, I think, was

God's way of saying, "Don't worry; I got this." That's largely why I chose the name "Trinity." Girlfriend clearly had supernatural connections. During my pregnancy I was terror-stricken at the thought of having a second daughter. There was, of course, the obvious: having to raise up yet another woman. But on top of that daunting anxiety, I had to steer the whole sister thing—that primitive and peculiar dynamic between potential female rivals. As all women, especially black women, know, there are sisters and then there are *SISTAHS*. I had to help these two baby girls grow into both. I felt that I had to somehow learn to rear them to be solid, supportive sisters to each other as well as womankind. I know all siblings have to deal with comparisons and petty jealousies. It just seems—as with most things—being black makes for a few additional complications. I mean, even if my two baby girls grew up to love each other like cooked food, there would be no way for me to shield them from certain occupational hazards.

For starters: The Whispers of Other Black Folks.

For all y'all who don't know, this is how it goes. Inevitably when the baby comes home and meets extended family, there is a conversation like this:

BLACK RELATIVE NUMBER ONE: "Oooh! She's just as pretty as can be!"

BLACK RELATIVE NUMBER TWO: "Uh-huh . . . isn't she though? Looks a little like Aunt [fill in the blank]."

BLACK RELATIVE NUMBER ONE: "Yep, I see it. Right around the eyes."

BLACK RELATIVE NUMBER TWO: "You see what's happening with her earlobes, don't you? She won't be high yellow for long. I tell you that."

BLACK RELATIVE NUMBER ONE: "Sho' nuff. She'll be complected like her daddy's side."

For sure, there are some black people reading this who would like to pretend this conversation doesn't go on in *their* family. I have two words: "Stop lying!"

Whether you hear them spoken or not, someone among your kinfolk is uttering words strikingly similar to these—and, if not, they are thinking them. For now, to spare those readers who have never seen or heard of hot combs or bergamot grease—and in deference to those for whom Rihanna's crystal-studded doobie at the American Music Awards was a trendy new hairstyle—I'm going to table the conversation "your mama and them" usually have about babies' hair texture.

My own mama was unabashedly taken with Trinity's crinkle-free newborn locks. For weeks upon weeks, wash after wash, my child's hair clung to her scalp without so much as a passing nod to the motherland. It was bone straight. There was no curl, no wave. Nothing but slick-back—picture the modern-day Al Sharpton, camera-ready after a fresh touch-up and press-set with pomade. For us black chicks, hair is life. I needed some kink up in there somewhere.

Maybe it was the raging postdelivery hormones, but almost everything in my babies' first few weeks of life caused me major angst. For example, I was certain that Trinity's protruding belly button was not just an outie but a severe umbilical hernia (which I learned of after one of my many "worst-case scenario" Google searches). My pediatrician and I nearly came to blows when she didn't see the urgent need for a surgical specialist. I was almost certain Trinity's "birth defect" was tied to Mark's handling on her born day. The nurses allowed him to cut the umbilical cord, after all, so he was the last person to touch it.

If I was so upset by her navel (consider her plight, for God's sake, if the early-nineties midriff made a come-back!), you can only imagine the consternation her hair caused me. My baby's tresses had me stressing. I began to pray for kinks—day and night.

For black women, hair is not just something that grows out of your head. In many ways, it can define your place in the world. Now don't shoot the messenger; I'm just being

honest. Many of us struggle into adulthood with hair issues. Here's the thing: I wanted Trinity's hair to be pretty.
To my mind, that would be one less thing for her to worry
about. It was a given that at some point she'd have to grap-
ple what I call the Three B's of becoming a young woman:
Booty, Boobs, and Bearing—though not necessarily in
that order and by no means limited to these three areas.

For me, booty—or the lack thereof—was one of the
first orders of adolescent business. Mama sent us to Cath-
olic school; I started to notice that not everyone's uniform
lay flat in the back, as mine did. When Wanda and Darlene walked up to the blackboard, their skirts danced in a
rhythmic back-and-forth motion, giving them a womanly
swagger I craved. For months I worked to emulate the gait
that sent the blue and green plaid print a-flapping, but I
could never quite perfect it. And the effort was draining.
Then it hit me: What Wanda and Darlene and them had
going on was not a practiced strut; it was a big butt. I
thought all that booty was a handy accessory, but they
hated carrying all that trunk junk. They lamented the fact
that boys and men stared at it all the time. Same with
boobs—because, as you may have guessed, Darlene and
Wanda were the first bra-wearers in my crew.

Few of us are completely happy with our booties and
boobies, especially early on. Suffice it to say, everything

about our bodies is "too" something. So we wait. We reach womanhood and go out into the world—praying that Spanx, underwire, and a little help from Victoria will keep our secrets.

But then that's just the outside. I thought, if my daughters' lives were anything like mine, the third B would pose even bigger problems. See, as it just so happens, I move about the world with a certain Bearing that often seems to confound folks. I appear supremely confident to most (I'm really not). I've been told I have a proud air (that one is true). Some call it regal (thing is, I have a freakishly long neck—and Mama always made me stand straight).

As a young girl, I also got plenty of unkind observations like "stuck-up" and "she think she cute." To make matters even more vexing for my detractors, I have joy. That's not to say I am always happy. I get mad, sad, and everything else that normal people experience. But it doesn't stick for some reason—at least not on the outside. Inside is a whole 'nuther story, but I am my mama's child. I just wasn't raised to put everything out on display. If you ever get to a black church, I guarantee an old woman will get up and end her testimony by saying: "Thank God I don't look like what I been through." That's me. Oh, and I laugh loud and often. In fact, I crack myself up. I'm kind of crazy but I'm far from stupid. And some people don't quite know what to make of that.

Now all this may seem unimportant, but it is no small matter. In my experience (and I have been walking the earth forty-odd years), people like to be able to put a woman—especially a black woman—in a slot. Is she Aunt Jemima? Is she bookish? Is she angry? Is she slutty? People don't like it when they can't figure you out. It's not enough for most women to just "be." Despite Yoncey's claim that "girls run the world," sadly we don't. Men do. So then we have to learn how to conduct ourselves in the world in a way that gets us noticed enough to nab the coveted scholarship or promotion—but not so noticed that we pose a threat. We've gotta grab the attention of the men who hold power, but not so much that they end up grabbing on us. We have to find a way to show off our smarts without being seen as show-offs. But then—and here's the rub—most decision makers, whether they are men or women, have a love-hate relationship with smart women. As Run-DMC will attest, "It's tricky" for sisters like me. We have to dance a dicey two-step to pepper meetings with just enough intelligence to keep things stimulating but not so much that a potential boss might find you intimidating.

Rightly or wrongly, I reckoned my girls would face the same issues. And since I brought her into this world— sorta, kinda, if you downplay the way she bolted out of me—I wanted Trinity, both my daughters, to have an easier life than mine. All mothers want that for their children. My black woman-child did not need one more ingredient for the world to stir into its already ample jug of hater-ade.

I've got to keep it real—this hair thing could totally tip the scales against Baby Girl and jack up her future. Important, it could also lead to an identity—not to mention—fashion crisis. Seriously, what does straight hair even *do*? Just lies down all the time with no sass, no point of view. That's not my child. She may be only weeks old, but she is no milquetoast kind of girl. Besides, for the better part of my adulthood, I myself had been rocking my natural-born naps (with varying degrees of "texturizing" success). And I rather liked it. As my offspring, it seemed only right that Trinity look as though she actually shared my DNA. I know it seems shallow, but I'm just keeping it real. I didn't want to be one of those mothers pushing their baby in the stroller only to be asked, "Are you the nanny?" Straight, white-looking hair would be a problem. Okay?

Thank heaven that the coarse and exceedingly dominant Mandingo genes from my side of the family prevailed. Slowly but surely, my baby's hair started to thicken and curl quite nicely—thank you very much. Beyond her tresses, Trinity surprised me in all kinds of ways. I'm not certain if I was simply more relaxed this second time around or if she was a super-easy kid.

But let me just say this: Homegirl latched on like a professional baby. No nudging, no prodding. Hurtling through a birth canal probably takes a lot out of a tiny little sister, because Trinity was beyond hungry; she was "howngry," nursing about five seconds after she arrived. For me, the deal was sealed right then and there. Clearly she was a prodigy. Two hours old, already she was smarter than her big sister.

Truth be told, I did not have high expectations for her. Okay, I had none. Since this was not my first time at the rodeo, I told myself I had to release them all so as not to project too much of Chloe onto her little sister. You have no idea how hard I had to work, over the course of nine months, to banish Sade ("never as good as the first time . . .") out of my head. Luckily, Trinity more than held her own.

The notion of a second-born holds little intrinsic delight and wonder. Frankly, the first one steals so many *ooohs* and *aaaahs*, you wonder deep down if you have any more left. From the outset, the entire pregnancy had an emotional "been-there-done-that" vibe cast on the whole experience. And with kids close in age, like my Chloe and Trinity, the physical challenges are far greater. At least with baby number one, when you get that bone-tired feeling you can simply lie down. Not the second time around.

The built-in limitations of pregnancy were made worse by the fact that—in my infinite wisdom—I'd accepted an exciting new job in my seventh month.

First, the good news: After a year or so of scratching up freelance work hither and yon, I'd managed to fall into a dream gig. As fate would have it, I nailed a plum assignment at *Essence* at a time when the magazine was in the middle of major changes. At the helm, spearheading the new direction, was Monique Greenwood, *Essence*'s newly named editor-in-chief—a longtime mentor and sister-friend to the fullest who decided to bring me aboard. It was an unlikely career coup for me to have landed on the masthead of the world's premiere publication for black women. It's not that I lacked talent or qualification, but I'm pretty sure *Essence* is a club to which I'd otherwise never have won admittance.

If you promise to keep it on the low, I will let you in on a little secret: Back in the day, there were some quarters where I was not always considered "black enough." Now, I'm plenty black. I can dance. I am fluent in Ebonics. And when pressed, I can throw my hand on my hip, roll my eyes, and snap my neck *AT THE SAME DAMN TIME*! It may have something to do with the whole "you think you cute" thing I told you about earlier. But the perceived "lack of black" started in high school, I think, because I was equally cool with Emily and her crew as I was with Bonita and hers. Then in college, I had the unmitigated gall to sit in the cafeteria anywhere I good and well pleased, sometimes with lots of white folks, sometimes with lots of football players—instead of with the thirsty wannabe "revolutionaries"—and it seemed to dog me for quite some time.

I digress. The bottom line was I'd scored a dream job, despite my questionable pedigree.

Now, the not-so-good news: Note to self—the middle part of a pregnant woman's third trimester is not an ideal time to begin anything more demanding than a power nap, especially if—as in my case—she is concurrently navigating the terrible twos. Like lumbering down Seventh Avenue and plodding up a flight of stairs toward Seven Nails, I probably had no business launching into a full-blown career ascent at that particular juncture in life. On my best days, mornings and evenings found me racewalking along Seventh Avenue brandishing a Maclaren power-wheel stroller to get Chloe to and from daycare before hightailing it up the subway stairs. On bad days, my neighbors saw me bolting down the street like an Olympic sprinter carrying a large basketball under her blouse. Now that I think about it, no wonder Trinity charged out of my body like a blazing shot put; I'd given her lots of track-and-field practice. On my worst days, I arrived at daycare a few minutes past the six o'clock pickup time, catching

Chloe's dejected, pooh-pooh face and the side-eye from her disapproving caregivers.

At a time when most women in my condition would've been in a nesting state, I was living in a state of frenzied panic—rushing to daycare, to the train, to Midtown Manhattan. It was also lonely, because Mark was in a new state as well—having just accepted a job working in New Jersey. The long commute to and from Park Slope, Brooklyn, meant he left home early in the morning and didn't get back until late in the evening. I was essentially a single mom.

To this day, I am not exactly sure how or when we decided to look for a house in New Jersey. I began to meet other moms who'd decided to brave this faraway land just west of New York City. I'd heard of one family that set out across the Hudson from Prospect Heights—with little more than some Ikea furniture, a cramped Subaru, and some Annie's organics—in search of a driveway, decent school district, and freedom from coin-op laundries. They made it safely, according to late-nineties folklore, to a three-bedroom, two-bath, center-hall Colonial. They happily settled along the frontier and, after brave exploration, discovered a Starbucks in the nearby wilderness.

I caught hold of that pioneering spirit. Soon Mark and I were spending weekends scouring real estate sites and fighting Lincoln Tunnel traffic to get to open houses. In retrospect, we (and millions like us) were part of the giant housing spit bubble just frothing at the corner of the economy. Once we decided in earnest to go west and put down stakes in Tony Soprano territory, our modest Park Slope co-op sold, and sold quickly for about 150 percent more than we'd paid for it five years prior. For all of about five minutes I felt like I was in that skit from *The Dave Chappelle Show*, yelling: "I'm rich, *biatch*!"

Then the crazy, nasty, bidding-war truth set in. And we realized that our royal flush was but a baby. After several disappointments, our offer on a house was accepted. It was a Dream Home for Mark and the real estate broker, who loved the home for its sprawling backyard (that I could never really see us using very much). For me, it was not so much a Dream Home as it was what I call an Imagine Home—as in, "Imagine this joint if the 1970s called and took back its linoleum floors, Formica shelving, and faux wood paneling." But at nine months pregnant and effectively homeless, I'd reached the point where charm, character, and other froufrou elements were no longer required; four walls and a roof were my only must-haves.

With a baby and a major move looming (possibly even converging; Trinity was due within days of our scheduled closing), I did what any capable, grown woman would do. I called my mama. But not right away. I thought about it—long and hard.

Doing so brought up some brutal realities of the past two years that I hadn't yet dared admit. Neither of us had really adjusted very well to the new dynamic that Chloe had thrown into our relationship. Obviously, we were mother and daughter. But we were also both moms now—and each of us had pretty strong opinions. It was, perhaps, a bit bratty of me to hold on to the past. But truth be told, I was still stewing over the fact that Mama had bailed on me in those early weeks of motherhood. Mama should've known how hard life with a newborn would get three or four weeks in. I mean, she was the one always going on about her in-depth knowledge of all things baby. If she really just had to go, why not cook and freeze a few meals? Help a sister out?

Mama did eventually return to help out with Chloe a couple of months later. But when she blew back into town, the effect was even more painful. I was expecting a gentle wind of relief, and instead I felt like I'd gotten more of a blustery gust of criticism and scorn. We never talked about it. And in the months that followed, we'd had a few frosty exchanges. Sometimes I was the one throwing shade—like the time during one of her visits that I angrily insisted on turning off the TV show Mama was watching because it would ostensibly hurt Chloe's eyes. Then there was that holiday visit to Buffalo when Mama wished me a Happy New Year, then added laughingly, but seriously, in that way mothers are trained to do: "I love you, but I love my grandbaby more!"

That really stung. Certain things are probably better left unsaid. Besides, Mama and I were not in a light, jokey-joke place right then. Far from it.

Despite our less-than-perfectness in that particular space, there was no one else I wanted beside me in a pinch. And this, I feared, would be a pinch if there ever was one. In scant weeks, I was going to have to pack up our three-bedroom apartment, move to another state, unpack, make house, go on maternity leave, find Chloe a preschool, hire a New Jersey babysitter—oh, and, of course, give birth to the new baby. Did I mention that this all needed to happen at Christmastime?

Phoning Mama did not go according to plan. With my crazy self, I thought I'd lay out the tasks in front of me and Mama would say something like, "How can I help?" I'm just wacky like that, I guess. The way I'd played out the conversation in my head, Mama would jet from Buffalo to Brooklyn after Trinity was born. That way, she could hang out with Chloe and play backup as I got things organized for the move.

Turns out, Mama thought it best to visit before Trinity was born and stay a little while as I settled in after the delivery. She explained how much more smoothly things would go if she were around to take Chloe to daycare, help out around the house, and take care of the new baby. The only problem with her plan was that this was not what I needed her to do. First off, I seemed to be supremely accomplished when it came to birthing babies. There would be no "recuperating"; I'd have the baby and keep stepping. With my newborn neatly tucked in a baby carrier inside my coat, I would stroll Chloe to and from school. End of story.

That was the least of my worries. After dancing around for a bit, sort of placating each other with subtle debate, I'd had enough of Mama defining "help" for me. There were plenty of sitters in my Rolodex who could "help" in the way she was proposing. Besides, Chloe had little toddler friends, and those toddler friends had moms with whom I was friendly. There's this thing, I tried to tell Mama, people do now, called playdates. There would be no time for cooing and playing patty-cake. We'd be closing on both the apartment and the house. I needed someone to help me bust a move!

My patience was thin. With an admittedly ill-mannered bite to my tone, I said: "I tell you what. Let's not call it 'help.' Okay? Why don't we just say you are coming to do whatever it is you want to do. Because clearly if what I need you to do doesn't fit *your* agenda, I'm on my own here. Right?"

After each syllable, I could almost feel blood on my tongue as I clipped the consonants with stinging sarcasm. My words were so sharp that I might as well have cursed Mama out. Never in my days had I spoken to her like that. I was so mad and so frustrated I had to hold back my tears. I didn't want to cry—although the hurt had been waiting to come out for a long time—because I needed Mama to feel my fury, not my pain. She wouldn't get that part anyway, I told myself. She never did.

There was no way Mama was backing down. She slammed back and said I was selfish, which I'm sure I disputed. Harshly. Vehemently. Self-righteously. But looking back, I would have to agree to a certain extent. I was entitled, to my way of thinking, to have Mama drop everything and do as I said when I said.

Now with three kids of my own, I can imagine how Mama must've felt. She'd raised me, fed me, loved me, put me through school, supported me. She didn't owe me anything. I'm not saying it wouldn't have been nice to have Mama's undivided attention. I did want that. And, at the time, I felt I deserved it. But in truth, Mama had never given me cause to expect it. I was acting out of some delusional sense of what I thought Mama should be—not who she was.

As I struggled through those first few weeks of motherhood, my sister reported that Mama had called her in exasperation one night to say: "I don't know about your little sister with all this whining. . . . She's just going to have to get it together. Hell, *I* did."

Ouch! Mama's backbiting was an open secret in our family. And although her remarks cut me down to the white meat, they were more of a confirmation than a condemnation. Mama was being Mama. And you know what? I needed to *mom up.*

CHAPTER SIX

Gotta Fight the Power
That Be

Before notable distinctions like the invention of Buffalo chicken wings and birthing Rick James, my hometown was far more than the butt of late-night jokes. In the 1950s, when my parents and tons of other black folks trekked up from the South, it was a very happening scene—with a population bloated to nearly six hundred thousand and plenty of jobs in transportation and manufacturing. Just a decade or so later, Buffalo started on a steady decline.

Like every grown-up I knew, Mama worked hard. She sometimes worked the night shift, three P.M. till midnight. It wasn't all that bad. If I raced home from school—I'm talking quick-fast, running like I stole something—I got to spend about fifteen or twenty uninterrupted minutes alone in her company as she prepared for the windshield wiper factory. We all know that it is not easy for a kid to beat back distractions. But I was determined. After school I had to will myself to cut a path to our front door. That meant:

- No stopping at the store for penny candy (chewy Mary Janes and Bazooka bubble gum were my everything)
- No walking a half block out of the way to dish with my best friend, Patrick—whom I so admired for being big and bad in the face of older boys who mockingly called him Patty ("Forget you, June Bug!" he'd shout with righteous indignation)
- And the really, really hard one—no circling around Punkin-and-them playing the dozens to an instigating audience of fourth- and fifth-graders—yelling "Ooooooh!" and "He talkin' bout your mama!"

All of these pleasures paled in comparison to the joy that awaited me. Once I spilled into the house, I'd find Mama in one of two places: If she was running behind schedule, she was in our tiny bathroom feverishly spraying Afro Sheen all over her Coffy-esque bush wig—with her just-pressed bell-bottom jeans hanging on the door hook. This was rare and not ideal. Since we didn't have a car at the time, Mama caught rides with Willie-Mae and other friends. They liked to arrive with enough time to relax before punching in. She hated running late.

More often, by the time I arrived Mama would be chilling on our red living room sofa. It was somewhat fancy—a brocade pattern—French Provincial, she said. Mama didn't go for plastic covering, rather believed we kids should be "trained" to be mindful. We were allowed to sit on the sofa, but not to "plop" upon it. The nuance was not lost on me during these still moments of our special afternoons. I was on my best behavior. No plopping. No hollering. In fact, I rarely spoke. Just listened. I'd sit with Mama as she drank her coffee (no sugar, no cream) and began the ritualistic tasks as prelude for the factory—patiently outlining the details of the job.

See, there were "office" politics at play at the plant. And as best she could, Mama mapped them out for me. She never said in so many words, but I got the impression that all of her bosses were men. I would venture to guess further that they were all mostly white men.

Let's just say that Mama was no stranger to certain power dynamics—racial and otherwise. No slight goes unnoticed. Once we were in a nice department store to buy Easter clothes when a perky saleslady approached. "What can I do for you girls today?" she chirped. To my five-year-old ears, the woman seemed just lovely. But

Mama shot her a glare something fierce and snapped: "I don't see but one girl and she does not have a pocketbook. I'll be taking mine elsewhere." I was mortified and utterly confounded. Here was this well-meaning saleslady who'd taken the time to lay her blue-shadowed eyes on us really nice-like. Why did Mama have to go and spoil the moment? This was a very fancy store. It was quiet. There were no rows of checkout counters—like Twin Fair, where we usually shopped. Soft music, probably Captain and Tennille's "Muskrat Love," was humming in the background. And here was Mama—finna take off her earrings and throw down.

It was clear from the way she was squinting her eyes that Mama was *this* close to cussing, something I'd rarely witnessed in public. Instead she turned on her heel and headed toward the door. I had no choice but to follow as Mama stormed out of the store. She was fired up. After a while I got angry too. Moments into the girls' dress department, I'd spotted a powder blue ensemble on one of the racks that had my name all over it. We rode the bus home in steamy silence.

I got the impression from the way she talked about the factory that some of the same forces that rankled her that fateful afternoon were at play with her supervisors. She spoke often of the important role of the union. How tonight she might have to report the foreman if he tried to get her to do something dangerous or outside her grade. Of course, she had no problem setting the foreman straight. She told me she didn't need to raise her voice or curse him out. All she had to say was, "No, I won't be doing that. I know my rights."

Mama needed to unwind at home because she would be standing for long hours on an assembly line. Naturally I pictured Lucy and Ethel cutting up at the chocolate factory. But she explained to me that in real life, factory work was neither sweet nor funny. Mama never groused about the difficulties or dangers. But it was clear to me, on some level, that it must've been a bit precarious. When she was on second-shift duty, there were different steps added to her at-home routine. She'd put balled-up cotton in her ears, for example. She drank more coffee than usual. And then came the good part—where I came in. Mama would get a roll of white adhesive tape—the kind found in most first-aid kits. And she'd begin cutting long strips to swath around her fingers and thumbs. I didn't get to handle the scissors as much as I might've liked. But I was allowed to let the strips hang from my own ten little fingers—enough to pretend I had really long, grown-up nails—while Mama wrapped and wrapped like a prizefighter, to the point where her fingertips looked as though there were fat bowl-like nubs attached to them. A lot of people don't realize that windshield wipers are pretty sharp. And as they come across the belt, faster and faster—the conveyor was indeed much like the one depicted on *I Love Lucy*—the parts were perilously sharp.

The radio played throughout the house. Mama was challenged not only by dance rhythms; she also seemed to have difficulty with melodic sounds. My siblings and I were convinced she was tone deaf. But Mama did love her jams. Back then, the Isley Brothers were putting it down. *"It's your thing. Do what you wanna do. I can't tell ya who to sock it to!"* she'd sing—loudly and off-key, as we sat deeply focused on these important prework procedures. Nothing spectacular took place. And I suppose that was the beauty of it. Once done, Mama gave me a quick kiss and she was out the door. Right about then, I would usually grab my favorite after-school snack—a bowl of Trix cereal—and settle in to watch *The Mike Douglas Show*.

We had one of those large TV–record player combo consoles that sat prominently in our living room. It was a big-screen, stereo viewing experience. I didn't get the jokes very often. But I really enjoyed the way Mike, with his soothing voice and those snazzy brown-beige suits, got to sit around chilling with all kinds of fascinating people.

It was on *The Mike Douglas Show*, if memory serves me correctly, that I caught my first glimpse of the Staple Singers. There was an old man strumming a very funky guitar, and several old—though slightly less old—women, singing over and over again: *"I'll take you there . . ."* I'd never seen old people so cool. My grandfather lived with us back then. I loved Papa a whole lot, but *cool* was not a word I'd use to describe the handsome suspendered man who looked after me in Mama's absence each day. He was enchanted by my every move—as though I were the sun, moon, and stars. And in that precocious way of little girls who operate with full knowledge that adoring eyes are upon them, I did my level best to wrap Papa around my fingers at every turn. Lovingly, of course, because the bond we shared was so powerful I wanted nothing more than to see delight in his eyes. I mimicked him tirelessly. Whether he was taken with the Staple Singers' chorus or the blues guitar solo remains a mystery, but Papa swiftly emerged from his bedroom, settled down into the coordinating brocade chair across from the sofa, and set his bespectacled gaze on the TV—smiling. Seemingly out of nowhere, Mavis began to wail: *"Aaaah . . . Aaaah . . . Aaaah . . . Oh, Aaaah. I know a place, y'all . . . Ain't nobody crying. Ain't nobody worried . . ."*

I had no earthly idea where the Staple Singers were planning to take me, but I was as moved by the words of the song as I was the gospel delivery, imagining that they must've been referring to Fantasy Island or some other exotic attraction. Papa liked it too, but he was apparently hearing something different in his ears. I saw that his eyes were closed and in a voice very quiet like he kept saying, "Have mercy" as though it were Sunday morning—not Tuesday afternoon—and he was perched in a pew up in Antioch Baptist Church. Papa demanded unconditional reverence of two things: Walter Cronkite and the Holy Ghost. I dare not speak.

Times change. When my kids were young and impressionable like I was back then, they did not witness a soulful prelude to my workday so much as a frenetic mix tape. Preparing for work, as a modern mother with small children, didn't mean getting ready so much as getting outta the house. Success meant that my feet had managed to cross the threshold from my front hallway onto the cemented ground of the outdoors.

Nothing in my routine was tranquil or meticulous. For example, my 'do was not tight—not done right. My goals were far more modest—clean drawers and deodorant. Usually I was in some varied state of undress—skirt twisted, bra strap slipped, a fly unzipped. Always the hair was still wet—that was a given. Makeup application was a luxury I could not afford; it would have to wait until I settled in my seat, if I got one—somewhere along Route 3, next to the unlucky soul forced to share tight commuting quarters with a blush brush–wielding sister unabashedly beating her face so wildly that reddish-brown powdery droplets casually danced across his *New York Times*.

The everyday niceties of womanly charm and preparation took a backseat to my reality. When I started the day, chief among my considerations were all the things I had to remember not to forget—manuscripts, story pitches, nursing pads, and, most important, my Pump In Style. It was the mother of all breast pumps and beyond valuable. But despite its name, the bulky machine failed to add any fresh-to-def appeal to my outfits. And in hindsight I'm not certain my titties really required the industrial, professional-grade strength of its high-performance Swiss engineering. But that ten-pound bad boy was my constant companion.

For me, motherhood and work never seemed to mesh in quite the same way they did for Mama. Childcare most always meant drama for me. I don't know what it feels like to get up and go to work and not wonder or worry about my kids. As much as she loves her grandchildren, Mama is not trying to leave her house for mine to help tend to the kids. She has her reasons, all of them valid. I think what's left unspoken, though, is that borderline maniacal involvement in kids' worlds is anathema to her and other mothers of her generation. She sort of gets it, especially as her grandkids have grown older and she has seen phenomena like social media take over.

That's not even the half of it. At times, I still find myself struggling to explain to Mama that a typical workday does not automatically halt seven hours and fifty-nine minutes after it began. She will often say, "Don't you get off at five?" Mama doesn't understand how or why anyone would be at a job late into the evening or on weekends. In her day, the union rep came to the defense of workers. Fair was fair.

Without coming right out and saying it, Mama seems to be convinced that I have the ability or the power to stop working at an appointed hour, as though a Bedrock-like steam horn blows through the office to announce quitting time and we do a Fred-Flintstone-Barney-Rubble scurry to the homestead for dinner.

I've stopped trying to explain that work is just different now. Of course, I am grateful. Mama's taped-up digits did not toil in vain. Her dream was that I'd never have to experience the capricious demands of a line foreman.

Since, thanks to Mama, I had a better life than she'd had. Since, as Nina Simone sang, I was young, gifted, and black. Since my college degree spared me the dangers of an assembly line. Since, on paper, I was an equal partner in my marriage. Since two middle(ish)-class incomes had afforded us a house in the suburbs. Since I was smart and ambitious. Since I was a woman and worked in the world of women's magazines. Since so many things were in my favor, I often wondered, why didn't my work life seem to work?

Maybe I was in the wrong field. Maybe I wasn't a team player. I love that term. It's supervisor code-speak for "We don't like you." Every time I hear it, I've had to beat back the urge to scream, "I know I'm not a team player because your team sucks!" One boss at a popular women's monthly had, in her own feckless way, tried to explain what she meant. She'd called me into her office to discuss the four-day work schedule I'd negotiated with her predecessor. In her view my workweek—prorated, mind you—was a "real sweetheart deal." Careerwise, she'd said, I was shooting myself in the foot, because while my colleagues "worked like beavers," I was at home. She suggested that I was already at a disadvantage because I had young kids. And she kept saying, "You *knoooow?*" and *"Okaaaaay?"* Her brows were furrowed and she was trying to either summon a smile or adjust her dentures. I just remember that throughout the spiel an awkward grin kept flashing across her face, and they seemed oddly timed. Then she referenced the week prior when I'd left work for an emergency at home. Trinity, who'd just started walking, had fallen. With the single tooth my baby had at the time, she'd split her bottom lip—blood gushing. The editor capped the most discriminatory line of talk I'd ever heard with these words: "See what I *meeeeean?* Swollen lips, ear infections, fevers—for you, there's always going to be something. You *knoooow?*"

In fairness to this woman, let me say this. I may have

unwittingly revealed my opinion of her journalistic heft the day we met. See, this boss fancied herself an intellectual and literary genius of sorts. She wasn't. Full disclosure: I was not happy to see her replace the beloved editor-in-chief who'd hired me and many others in an attempt to freshen the tired publication. Even fuller disclosure: I was skeptical upon first laying eyes on her when the new editor held court, introducing herself to the entire staff, wearing peep-toe shoes—a style choice that couldn't help but expose the hard evidence of tragically chipped, weeks-old toenail polish that had been haphazardly painted over.

Is that petty of me? I'm sorry. I think not. It speaks to larger issues like conscientiousness and integrity. I mean it. Mama used to chastise us for even the smallest half-truth. "If you'll lie, you'll steal!" she yelled. By the same token, if you are shady enough to try to cover up a derelict pedicure, what else will you scheme? It was a Monday, for goodness' sake. The woman had all weekend to freshen that coat. Why not remove all remnants of crumbling shellac and simply come clean? That, I could respect. Disclosure to the fullest: I didn't much like her.

Sadly, her duplicitous kind had plenty of company in the hallowed halls of sisterhood. Another leading editor, given to rhapsodizing about our mandate to help improve the lives of our readers, talked incessantly about how long and hard she worked—suggesting in backhanded ways that, perhaps, some of us were less committed than she. Even as a young mother, she boasted, it was not uncommon for her to work through the night. How this improved the lives of our readers—not to mention the life of her daughter—was never clearly spelled out.

More than one of the editors who outranked me would use their best girlfriend tones to cross the legal boundaries of employer-employee relations. Not long after Trinity was born, they'd ask, "How's Mommy?" like my government name no longer fit. It irked me, and I never quite knew how to respond. I told myself they were probably just making small talk. See, I desperately wanted to believe that my "sisters" were good and honorable women. One morning a colleague was riding up in the elevator with me when the boss slipped in the closing doors. She smiled brightly at my childless associate. Then looked at me—my work case and breast pump crowding the tight space. This was before the ubiquity of cell phones and other gadgets, back when elevators forced a level of human engagement. Although her teeth were showing, she wasn't giving me a smile so much as a mix of confusion and abject pity. She was staring, perhaps unwittingly, at my still-bulging postpartum midsection. Then she said, "Look at you!" By the way, that's usually something people say when they realize they have been looking at you far too long and in a weird way. "Are you done or will you go for another?"

I was speechless but tried to crack a smile. Once Boss Lady left the elevator, my colleague turned to me and, confirming my suspicion, said: "Dang, she all up in your uterus, huh?"

Women like my bossy-bosses didn't get women like me. I don't know if it was generational or what. They were throwback feminists whose attitudes seemed to say, "You've got kids . . . and?"

They'd been there and done that, after all, by themselves as single moms. Here I was married? Hell, they didn't *need* a man to raise their kids—now grown or nearly grown, who they had no shame admitting they were not on good terms with. They did it all (insert fist pump). They were "invincible-hear-me-roar" type of sisters—and they had the scars to prove it. Maybe that's why they were always pushing us editors to write about pain—bad breakups, office torment, fibroid agony, too-tight hair-weave torture (for real—I think that's a thing).

It's a wonder I didn't lose my mind. Because here's the rub: I generally don't do pain. Not that messed-up things don't happen in my life. I have my share of done-wrong woe. I cry and I bleed. But after a while a sister *gots* to move on! I can't get with the victim piece. I was beginning to realize some things about women's magazines. And many of those things didn't sit well with me. When you think about it, there is something wrong with an industry built on the notion that everything about its core customer needs changing, improving, analyzing, reimagining—*all* the time. The articles we edited fell into one of several categories:

- Why did my man leave me?
- How can I get a man?
- How can I keep a man?
- Why can't I be happy—although I have a man?
- How can I change my (hair, boobs, thighs, abs) to please my man?
- How can I love myself (because my man won't)?
- Am I good enough? Hold up, let me ask my man.

Don't misunderstand. I love a good man. They can be awfully nice to have around. And I'm down for introspection, self-evaluation, and all that. I am not one to walk around like my stuff don't stink. But "ENOUGH!"

Such is the world of women's magazines. I was beginning to question where—if anywhere—I fit into my chosen field. According to the company line, our mission was to support women, empower women, celebrate women, and all that rah-rah. But I felt as though I were setting women back a few decades with every feature. If I'm really a feminist, how can I, in good conscience, edit story after story telling women how to drive a man wild? As far as I'm concerned, men ought to get on the pole and try to excite *us*, especially given how hard we work. And how strong a black woman am I if I'm constantly pushing stories about what white people think of us? To my mind, us editors should be telling sisters quite the opposite. I'm not suggesting for a second that we are postracial. But c'mon peeps, this is not 1972. Instead of studying what white people think, say, or do, we should be telling black women: "Do *you*, boo! You are *all* that!"

Instead I'm sitting in meetings with self-appointed grand poobahs of black womanhood declaring that sisters' primary concerns are centered on a man . . . and, oh yeah, that we don't wear pink. I had to call on Mavis and Pops Staples in my head: *"Help me . . . Somebody. Somebody, help me now."*

CHAPTER SEVEN

Some Try to Fool You;
Some Try to School You

Mama had no problem with four-letter words. She would tell you—and the horse you rode in on—what you could do, where to go, and when. No questions asked.

But her make-it-happen, find-a-way-out-of-no-way survivor instincts left little room for the four-letter word I found myself needing most as a strange mom in a strange land: H-E-L-P.

A few weeks after we'd moved into our new suburban house, a tall brown-skinned woman arrived at the front step. Still on maternity leave, I was slowly growing accustomed to the parade of during-the-day door knockers who apparently rolled up in these parts when most people were grinding their nine-to-fives. Magazine subscription peddlers. Lawn service pushers. Charity hawkers. There was a steady stream of folks trolling the sidewalks.

I wasn't in the habit of answering the doorbell anytime

it rang. I guess I still had enough Brooklyn in me to be wary of the unannounced. From an upstairs window, I peeked down to get a better view. The woman had a large bag with her . . . white with red stripes, the kind sold at subway stops throughout the city that lots of people used to tote clothes back and forth to the Laundromat. I decided to go to the door. At least she wasn't a Jehovah's Witness. There was something about her face—though it was not the least bit friendly—that spoke to me, "like a letter from home," as Mama would say.

With a baby on my hip, I reached to unlock the stormer with my one free hand. She looked me up and down for what felt like five minutes. Then she said, "You must be the new housekeeper, huh?" I tried not to look offended. My hair was nappy. I wasn't wearing lipstick and I might have been wearing the clothes I slept in. But it's not like me and Hattie McDaniel could've passed for twins—at least I didn't think so. "No, I live here," I said. "This is my house."

She didn't apologize, as I recall . . . just made one of those "uh-huh" sounds, as many black women are wont to do when words can't do justice to their true feelings, and launched into her spiel. "Well, I clean for the people across the street and I used to clean this house too," she explained. "I know everything about this place. So if you need help or whatever, I do know what I'm doing. You can ask around if you don't believe me."

She didn't smile or make any attempt at warmth in her abrupt pitch. Not that I needed a song and dance. I just thought . . . Well, actually I don't know what I thought. I guess I didn't think anything because I'd never even considered hiring someone to clean my house.

It was my house, after all. My kids. My mess. And besides, who doesn't know how to clean? Mama made us scrub grout with toothbrushes. Mama had such standards, she made us scrub our sidewalk. She had solvents and solutions and potions and whatnot that she forced us to use in the garage. I assumed everyone grew up just as I did. A housekeeper? What in the world did I look like? Some clueless little housewife with no home training?

When I was growing up, my aunt Dot kept house for a white lady she referred to as Miss Ann. I didn't know it then, but that was just a sort of code—like Mister Charlie—older black people used for white females with a bit of power. As a kid, I didn't really know what Aunt Dot did when I'd overhear her bring up the name Miss Ann. But when Auntie came over to the house to play cards with the other grown-ups, Miss Ann and Mister Charlie would always come up—usually in the context of "The White Man" and "The Old Country." The latter referred to whatever part of the South one hailed from. In Mama's case it meant Alabama and Bull Connor. For others at the card table it was South Carolina. As for the former . . . well, I suppose The White Man part is obvious. I came to realize that they were not talking about any particular white man. Just THE white man. Even if it was plural—like, for example, politicians, union heads, storekeepers—it was still The White Man from whom Mama and our guests had escaped. I'd often heard Mama say that turning the other cheek was fine for Dr. King, but "I couldn't live with that prejudiced mess without blowing somebody's brains out." Everybody would laugh and nod in agreement and then Mama would add something like, "The nonviolence kids might be put in jail, but they'd have to put me up under the jail, cuz I'd knock the hell outta the sons of bitches!" Even in the late seventies, when they'd established lives up North, the way Mama and them told it The White Man was still a danger—always trying to keep The Black Man down. My one uncle, Jimmy Mo', had a way around The White Man, however. He worked for himself.

He was very proud. He carried himself like a businessman of sorts too, although he was usually dressed in coveralls. Jimmy Mo'—his government name was James Moore, but *Moe* is how everyone pronounced it; my dad and some others actually cut it down to two syllables, Jim-Mo—was married to Aunt Dot, Dad's sister. He was in the same line of business as Fred Sanford. But I never heard anybody call him a junk man to his face. And I was almost full-grown before the least bit of awkward cringe set in when he drove past me on the street, honking and waving hello. I swear his truck was held together with so much duct tape and plywood you could almost hear the twanging *Sanford and Son* theme song as Jimmy Mo' revved its engine.

There was no hint of shame to his game. No shuffling and no kowtowing when he drove into the fancy hood to pick up Aunt Dot from work. Back then, I imagined that maybe Miss Ann was The White Man's wife, a kindly woman with whom Aunt Dot visited. Aunt Dot was naturally sweet and loving. So it was no surprise to me that her Miss Ann seemed to treat her just fine. She often had new-looking clothes and housewares that were given to her. It wasn't until years later that I realized Aunt Dot was a housekeeper. So was my aunt Helen. But Auntie H, while kindly deep down, was far more outspoken than Aunt Dot. I'm certain she was good at her job, but she was not turning the corners of her mouth for just anybody, unless they'd earned it. She saw no need for pleasantries—much like the woman standing before me.

I sent Ms. Unfriendly on her way. "Thanks, I got this," I think I said. She shrugged in a way that seemed to say: "Suit yourself. No skin off my nose."

A month or so later I returned to work following my maternity leave. After much consternation, I'd hired a babysitter for the kids. Most all the nursery schools and daycares in town either were filled to capacity or had operating hours more befitting the schedule of stay-at-home moms than commuters. So I was forced to leave my children each day in the care of a veritable stranger—an agency-backed, background-checked stranger with lauding references, but a stranger nonetheless. The agency I used specialized in something called "nanny placement," according to the ad.

I was desperate. I'd gone through all of my Brooklyn contacts to no avail. I even had my Brooklyn sitter on the case for me. Verona Goulbourne was so good, my kid used to cry in the evenings when she left. I could say she was the black Mary Poppins. But that wouldn't do her justice. I think, actually, Mary Poppins was the white Verona.

I had no choice but to call the nanny finder's 800 number. And I was exceedingly discomfited by the predicament. Maybe it's too harsh a judgment, but I just feel very strongly that if you're not talking about the zaftig Brit on television, no one should use that N-word. *Nanny* sounds waaaay to close to the word *Mammy* for my liking. The fact that the woman running the agency was black rankled me even more. She sent over a woman with a long résumé and a string of references from all over town.

Her name was Shirley. She was Jamaican. And she smiled *all* the time. I'm talking the grinning-for-no-apparent-reason kind of smile. Once, immediately after she'd flashed me one of those Cheshire Cat grins as I left the house, I turned my head back to find Shirley scowling like a prune. I didn't trust her. And I didn't like or understand how every day when I came home my house smelled of Clorox bleach.

Now, I am a cleaner-upper through and through. Generally, a push broom and Lysol wipes are the way to my heart. She probably thought a clean-smelling house would make me happy. But instead, it made me wonder: "How in the world does she find time to clean *and* take care of a house full of babies?" It just can't be done. And upon close inspection, I soon discovered that Shirley only made the house *smell* clean. When you took the trash liner out of the garbage can? Dirt. When you lifted the sink mat or went to empty the dish drain? Scum. Worst of all, when you dismantled the high chair and removed the seat cushion? Gunk, crumbs, dried milk. My babies could've died of botulism, for God's sake!

Smiling Shirley was a sad excuse . . . with her kid-neglecting and halfway-cleaning self. The kind of thorough, Mama-like housecleaning I needed was far more than I could handle alone. It was all I could do to get home in time to relieve Shirley's trifling behind (she practically had one foot out the door as soon as I arrived each night), feed the kids, bathe them, and read a book.

So one day, I marched my happy hips across the street and asked after the grumpy lady. I decided I'd get a housekeeper to clean and have the sitter sit—not combine both jobs in one. Of course, I didn't really think through the economics of that argument. It's not like I was pulling down some great salary. But I was already physically pained each day as I left my babies with an ever-cheesing stranger.

Beverly, it turns out, had been watching Shirley from a perch on the top floor of the neighbor's house for a while. She was not impressed. I would later learn that Beverly didn't like Shirley, primarily because she was Jamaican— that's a thing for lots of black folks. But she raised some good points, mostly confirming my suspicions. "Your kids don't get enough fresh air, if you ask me," Beverly reported. "And when she does take them outside she barely plays with them. If you ask me, she's just going through the motions. I'm just saying."

Turns out, Shirley's motions included finding a new family to work for. I guess she was about as fond of me as I was her—simpering aside. Within a few weeks, Verona arranged for Tiffa, a woman fresh from Trinidad, to work for me. I told her from jump not to focus much on cleaning. As a result, I often came home to a mess in the evenings. She'd let teething biscuit remains, for example, cake up on the ExerSaucer all day. But everyone on the block—Beverly included—reported that she talked and played with my kids like a real mom would. "If you ask me, she is not all she seems," Beverly said. "But she does love on your kids."

Once Beverly began cleaning for me, my whole life changed. She was unlike any of the black folks I'd come across in New Jersey. She charged me a ridiculously low rate and sometimes offered to come whether I could pay her or not. I used to sneak grocery gift cards into her pockets when she wasn't looking. And I always tried to give her as much cash as I could spare for her birthday, Mother's Day, and Christmas. She appreciated it, but she didn't particularly like it—forcing me to endure long speeches about how I needed to learn to accept help without "throwing my little bit of money" around.

She seemed to enjoy coming to the house. And despite her modest means, which included a patchwork system of double couponing, bus passes, and Section 8 housing, she rarely arrived without a bag full of Dollar Store books, crayons, or craft items for the kids.

Among the many bags of cleanser, rags, and sponges she brought with her an eighties-era boom box that she plugged in with no hesitation the moment she settled in.

Depending on her mood, I could look forward to the Chi-Lites (*"Have you seen her? Tell me have you seen her?"*), Blue Magic (*"So let the sideshow begin . . . Hurry, hurry . . ."*) or Teddy Pendergrass (*"Close the door. Let me rub your back where you say it's sore . . ."*). Nobody loves a throwback like I love a throwback. But Beverly would be playing these seventies classics all the livelong day. That's because she usually started cleaning my house at around ten in the morning and was still cleaning at six in the evening. Trust me, it's not a big house.

Other days, Beverly might not be in an R&B groove. She might need to get revolutionary on somebody. She loved a conspiracy. I have no idea where or how she found her favorite talk-radio stations on the dial. But she did, and she liked to laugh and talk back to the talk-radio people as they spoke. Usually it was Al Sharpton. I'm talking the marching Al Sharpton. Pre–Jenny Craig and mainstream acceptance. She prided herself on being informed and quickly dismissed "ignorant, uppity Negroes who don't know what time it is," a label she was not shy about casting on visitors who came by my house when she was present. Once the person left, she might say: "Where you know that house Negro from?"

Beverly was serious about black pride. She boasted that her boom box was tuned to the same station in the homes of whites for whom she cleaned. "Only I turn it up louder," she noted. "I don't want them to get it twisted; just because I clean houses doesn't mean I'm docile." With or without Rev. Al and Company blaring the airwaves, *docile* is not a word anyone would use to describe Beverly. She was barely civil, unless she really liked you.

Fortunately, Beverly not only liked me. She loved me. It wasn't a warm and fuzzy kind of love, but it was love just the same. Some days she would arrive with news clippings because Beverly prided herself on reading everything. If there was a black woman featured or even mentioned in an article, she would burst into the house exclaiming, "Ylonda, you could do that." If any of my former bosses made a TV appearance or wrote a book, Beverly would say, "Oooh, I cannot wait for you to show them up." She had very unkind words for anyone who *might* have slighted me. Beverly had a toughness I'd never witnessed. She was like Mama on steroids. She didn't cuss much, but she had very sharp words at times and judgments against all kinds of people. She referred to the father of her children as a sperm donor and her parents as "the people who raised me."

But she carried around some heavy-duty pain—not just the kind they talk about in women's magazines. Her late son had passed away of complications from AIDS, and she cried each time his birthday came around, recalling how no one—not even the hospital workers—wanted to touch him as he lay dying. Beverly was also in physical pain every day. She suffered badly from asthma. But she insisted on using that strong ammonia-based cleanser in the bathroom. I don't know if she ever laughed heartier than when I bought an organic brand and suggested she try it—or, at the very least, a face mask. "You are a trip. You know that? This mess won't clean nothing." She limped, for reasons that were never made clear. And she didn't sleep well, she often told me.

She liked to laugh. And a lot of the time, I was the butt of her humor. Her deep affection for me was not always immediately clear, especially when she was schooling me like so: "Look here, I had one of those mini pizzas you've got in the freezer and it was terrible. You really ought to buy a different brand. I know your kids probably think they taste nasty." Or she'd offer up marital advice in this way: "You might not believe it to see me now, but I know how to keep a man. You have got to dress up a little bit *sometime*. What are you wearing?"

She often cautioned me about things that might come up with other housekeepers. She explained, for example, that I should never trust a housekeeper who didn't wipe down the windowsills—not just the outside, but the inside part between the screen and actual window. She'd say things like: "You don't know any better. I know you never had a housekeeper before, so there's a lot you don't know. You have to watch me very carefully. I'm setting the standard."

Beverly grew up in Newark and had lived in several towns over the years. And she enjoyed telling me that "the hood is the hood wherever you go and so are the hood rats; sometimes they just dress nicer." When she made these kinds of observations, she liked to say, "always remember" or "if you ask me." Some points were so important that Beverly emphasized them with both of her favorite phrases. For example, the big one: "Always remember you can never completely trust anybody—if you ask me."

Looking back, I think Beverly must've known she was dying. That must be why she was always pouring into me. She used to tell me about the fallouts she had with her kids. They were teenagers, so the issues sounded to me like typical adolescent fare—dating, grades, responsibility, and the like. When she'd relay the back-and-forth, she would usually say, "I try to tell them I won't always be around to show you right from wrong." I say the same thing to my kids, but when she said it I remember now that she often got choked up.

Every year when the summer started to wind down I'd get to thinking about Beverly's mid-September birthday.

She came to my house every other week, so I liked to time my birthday presents ahead of her big day, not on the tail end. I figured that way if she wanted to do something nice for herself she'd have a little extra cash in hand. While I was away a few days leading up to Labor Day, Beverly left a voice mail message. She said she'd stopped by to help me get organized around the house and was across the street at the neighbor's house, waiting for me. The next voice mail message said she was going to "head home and come back tomorrow."

The next day her daughter called to say Beverly had died in her sleep.

CHAPTER EIGHT

Oops! Upside the Head

Life in my new homeland across the Hudson got off to a rocky start. Commuting into the city was not as easy-peasy as folks had made it out to be. We'd chosen our town for its diversity, but my search for regular black folks often dead-ended with "bourgie" Negroes. And, if that weren't enough, although it was billed as the walkable suburb, I soon noticed that some of the streets up in this piece had nary a sidewalk, for God's sake. Still, after a year—or four or five—the culture shocks waned and I slowly began to adjust. Life here was looking up.

In 2006, just after Labor Day, Trinity joined the legit league of school-aged children, entering kindergarten and joining her third-grade sister, Chloe. At ages five and seven, they may have looked like little girls to the rest of the world. But for me—having juggled writing deadlines with naps and playdates for the past few years—kids who now fed themselves and left the house for an hours-long stretch were as good as grown.

As if on cue, the stars aligned that same month and I was called for a job with Hearst Magazines. On interview day the school drop-off routine was drama-free. No one forgot her lunch, threw a fit, or had a wardrobe malfunction. I could get ready in peace. The sun was shining. It was a good hair day, one on which the humidity had kindly acquiesced, lending more curl and less nap to my mass of kinky hair—to a decidedly sexy and polished effect. My outfit was a cheap-chic "collabo" of H&M, T.J.Maxx, and Banana Republic. Everything fit—no rising, no binding, no itching (except the skirt tags scraping against my waist; at $129 that joint was going back to the mall the next day). I'd taken the time to beat my face to near-perfection with department-store makeup: "natural" caramel bronzer, kohl gray smoky eyeliner, endless strokes of black mascara, and lip gloss so shiny my mouth could pass for polyurethane. As I caught my reflection in the hall mirror on my way out the door, I couldn't help myself. To no one in particular, I shouted: "I guess I got my swagger back!"

The commute into the city was a breeze. I was feeling all brand-new, which was only fitting, because Hearst Tower was also new. Forty-six-stories-of-late-modern-gleaming-steel-and-glass new. I rolled up in the windowed atrium and went up the escalator like I owned the joint. The architecturally heralded cascading waterfall whisked on either side of me, leaving a soft breeze in its wake. In my mind, my hair was blowing. It wasn't really, because my 'fro was too dense to flow in photo-shoot fashion. The point is, it *could* have been blowing—given my mood. If I had any regret at all it was only that I didn't have a hat to toss into the air, Mary Tyler Moore style. Instead, I just hummed a bar or two of my absolute favorite seventies theme song in my head ("*Well, it's you, girl, and you should know it!*").

Once I landed on the mezzanine level, I boarded one of those ear-popping express elevators to the twenty-second floor. You know, the ones that travel at the speed of sound?

I was anything but nervous. Still, my stomach danced as I soared up that fancy skyscraper. It was not airy, not fluttery or light—more like a churning than turning. *Nothing serious*, I told myself, *it's not like I'm about to throw up.* But it was just enough to blow my high.

Then and there I knew: I was a little bit pregnant. If you think there is no such thing as being a "little bit pregnant," you have probably never miscarried. Despite the queasiness in my stomach, in my head I convinced myself—at least for the moment—that I was not at all likely to be having a baby. My "scientific" reasoning went as follows:

a) At forty, any eggs left in my ovaries had hard-boiled.

b) Since Trinity was born, I'd had two failed pregnan-
    cies.

c) God was fully aware that my nerves, not to mention
    my finances and marriage, could barely withstand
    the two kids I already had.

The interview went okay, not great. That fleeting bout
of morning sickness took my head out of the game. Gone
were the pithy summaries of my prior experience. I was
now preoccupied and suddenly hyperaware of each movement of the gastrointestinal twerk dance shaking my insides. It certainly didn't help matters when my internal
monologue started to regress. A few minutes into the
meeting, I had Florida Evans railing in my brain: "DAMN,
DAAMN, DAAAAAMN!"

Then I started praying to God. Well, it was not exactly
praying. Although I did say the words *God*, *Lord*, *Sweet
Baby Jesus*, and *Lord Most High* over and over again—in
hindsight it was more like playing *Let's Make a Deal*. The
Big Guy and I were engaged in very high-level bartering
discussions. In exchange for taking this preggers sensation
away—pronto—I told him I would start being a *lot* more
grateful for all my blessings: food, shelter, strong teeth
and bones. I promised I would start going to church more
often *and* tithing. In fact, I would be holy all the time. My

near-addiction to Wendy "how you doin'?" Williams had to be a sin, I figured. So I'd change the radio dial. Maybe it was time to start answering the phone with "Praise the Lord" instead of "Hello?" I knew I would need to throw out all my Notorious B.I.G. CDs, and I vowed to put an end to my secret affair with that sexy, chocolate-coated brother from *The Wire* on HBO. Breaking things off with my TV dreamboat was going to be especially difficult. But I was desperate and nothing was off the table.

Weeks passed and still no visit from Aunt Flo, if you know what I mean. I'd decided that absolutely no one— not even Mark, my mother, or my sister—could know about this maybe-baby thing. Who knew, I rationalized, if there would even *be* a baby? I could miscarry any day now. Cramping could start up like the last couple of times and find me squatted over the toilet flushing a crimson tide. If that were the case, I'd rather just deal with it alone. I didn't want to endure everyone's pathetic attempts to comfort me. Mark would ask no less than fifty-eleven times a day what I wanted to eat and show up from work with surprise treats—ice cream, cookies, and the like. Mama would feel compelled to offer her catch-all tragedy explanation— "Everything happens for a reason." And, of course, well-meaning friends and acquaintances would shower me with unsolicited mood checks and furrowed brows of concern at every turn.

I'd been there, done that. And was in no mood to press Rewind. I could handle this on my own, I thought. Meanwhile, I soldiered through morning-noon-and-night sickness—which neither Chloe or Trinity ever troubled me with—and violent aversions to every food and odor imaginable. Even coffee, long my personal magic elixir, sent my insides topsy-turvy. A nauseated stomach was not the only upset. My stubborn state of denial helped create an unstable edge to my otherwise sunny disposition. In other words, I was as mean as the devil's mistress. I didn't want to be, but hiding and secret-keeping takes a lot of energy. And I guess it left me little bandwidth for much else.

I finally broke down and bought one of those at-home pregnancy tests. Hmmm . . . maybe a false positive, I told myself—then bought three more. Okay, breathe. When I "broke" the news to Mark, he was neither glad, nor sad, nor mad. He just sort of sighed, I think. Mama was over-the-moon excited, especially later when we found out it was a boy. And the girls were downright giddy.

I was alone in my funk—a recurring theme. It's not that I didn't want another baby. For years, I'd hoped to have three kids. But with the failed pregnancies, I'd given up on the idea. Who doesn't want a baby? What I didn't want was yet another miscarriage. And no matter how far my pregnancy progressed, I could not erase the thought of loss at some point. I was quietly preparing for what I thought was inevitable. And I didn't dare tell anyone the fear I was harboring. How could I?

Pregnancy is supposed to make everyone happy. People approach you all amped up. No one wants to talk about heartburn or constipation, let alone death. The assumption is automatically: You are *with* child; you will soon *have* child. To speak on anything other than sunshine, flowers, and new life would be ungrateful—ungodly even.

Once I got past the three-month mark, most of my worst-case-scenario anxieties should have subsided. They didn't. I endured all kinds of wild dreams about having Rosemary's Baby. After that phase ended, I worried about what would happen if I didn't make it to the hospital in time for delivery. I like to think of myself as intensely loyal. Skeptics might say I simply don't like change. Maybe a combination of the two led me to go back to my New York OB/GYN's office on Manhattan's Upper East Side. In the beginning of my pregnancy, when prenatal visits are scheduled monthly, it wasn't so bad: the commuter bus to Port Authority, the New York subway—the 7 at Times Square across town, to the 6 uptown—then a brisk fifteen-minute walk to York Avenue. It was worth it. I knew them, I reasoned. And they knew me. Knowing me meant they shared my concern of possibly giving birth somewhere along a Hudson River crossing. Rather than risk getting stuck on the GW Bridge or in the Lincoln Tunnel, the doctor thought it best that I be induced, a prospect that after having quick drug-free deliveries I just couldn't wrap my head around.

Lots of people think I'm super-strong when it comes to giving birth. But I rarely reveal the flip side: I am terrified of needles and drugs. Those fears, not bravery, kept me from even entertaining an epidural shot. Pitocin terrified me. The idea of being induced was one I couldn't deal with.

Fortunately, I didn't have to. About a week before my due date, during the early morning hours of a Wednesday in May, I was woken by some cramps in my side. It was time for the girls to get ready for school. I ignored the cramps at first, but they returned just a couple of minutes later. Then again . . . and again. Mark got the girls up and started to get ready for work as I lay still—waiting.

"I feel something. You shouldn't go to work today," I said softly.

Staring dead at me, a woman roughly 275 days pregnant with her third child, he goes, "Why? What do you mean?" I thought back to a conversation three days prior, thinking: "Do men ever listen?" We'd taken the girls for ice cream. And as we sat in Applegate Farms licking our cones, I said nostalgically: "This is probably our last time out, with just us four. Girls, in a few days our baby will be here."

All matter-of-fact-like, as though in utero activity were a subject he actually knew something about, Mark looked at me with screw-face doubt (a countenance he has spent the better part of our marriage perfecting) and countered, "Nah, we've got a while yet. I can't see it." There are times—many times—when you can almost hate the one you love. I'm thinking to myself: "Dude, you've been pregnant—like—how many times? Tell me this is another one of your jokey-jokes."

That morning, faced with Mr. Oblivious, I was reminded once again that grace is a powerful thing. Somehow, despite being pissed to the highest level of pissivity, I managed to remain calm, even as my labor intensified. I got myself showered and dressed and had Mark take the girls to school. By the time he returned, the pressure against my cervix had progressed from a bout of rigorous sparring to full-blown rope-a-dope. I needed to get to New York–Presbyterian—stat. Only one teensy consideration: Traffic would be jammed across all major roadways because, after all, we were smack in the middle of morning rush hour.

I resigned myself to the facts before me. Instead of worrying, I was too busy high-fiving myself in my head: "You're *not* crazy, no matter what folks say," I assured me. "Looks like this baby really will be born on a highway shoulder." Luckily I'd just watched a Baby Week marathon on Discovery Channel, with episodes like "I Didn't Know I Was Pregnant," "Top Most Shocking Births," and "Woman Has Baby in Her Pants." At least I had a reclining passenger seat (unlike the poor woman on a city bus); I figured this couldn't be so bad compared to the moms on TV.

Just as I'd begun to run a mental checklist of birthing accouterments on hand in our trusty crossover wagon—hand sanitizer (glove compartment); blankets (backseat); jumper cables, maybe to pinch the cord off? (trunk)—we were rounding York Avenue to the hospital's main entrance. I was about to burst and I knew it. Before the car could come to a complete stop at the valet booth, I'd plopped myself into one of several wheelchairs near the automatic doors. Mark ran nervously behind me and began to steer the bulky vehicle through the corridors like a flag-blind IndyCar driver. He pumped the brakes only twice—once to board the elevator to the seventh floor, then to check in at the labor and delivery desk, where I noticed a big clock that read 10:00. I don't recall exactly what happened next, but I can still hear Mark hollering something about his "wife," then adding words like *baby* and *ready*. One of the nurses on duty seemed to be yelling as well. I remember her talking to Mark—not to me—saying, "Okay, sir. We'll check to see how long . . ." I don't know exactly where she was going with that. But I screamed, *"NOW!"* And they all stopped what they were doing. She asked Mark, "Is this her first or second pregnancy?"

What, was I invisible? I screamed again, *"THIRD!"*

She directed Mark to push me to a room at the end of the hall. I don't know, to this day, what the room was used for. It wasn't a delivery room, but I mean there was a table or a bed in it, as well as some screens and such. I couldn't care less. With Mark and the nurse on either side of me, I took off my clothes and got hoisted onto the bed-table. I announced, to no one in particular, *"I need to push."*

And so I did. Cole, already crowning, came out with no delay.

The first thing I saw was the light. Not the Godlike peace and joy, although there was plenty of that. I mean Cole was very, very fair—with coloring that seemed ten shades lighter than I'd seen with the girls. His skin was pink. His hair was beigey-brown; his eyes, light gray. Never in my life had I been so happy to see a living, breathing creature. He had ten fingers and ten toes and weighed in at a healthy seven pounds. It was exactly 10:15 A.M.

I'm guessing that May 9, 2007, was a slow news day. This was back before people had things to talk about, like Kimye and catfights on *The Real Housewives*. Because the women in labor and delivery at New York Hospital were going on and on like I was the most exciting thing since the

Hubble Telescope. One of the best things about drive-by deliveries like Cole and Trinity is that since staffers are caught unawares, no hospital procedures are really in place. Instead of having your baby snatched five minutes after birth, you get to cuddle and hang out with your newborn while they scramble to set up gadgets and processes.

The downside, in a way, is that you have to listen to a lot of watercooler back-and-forth. It's a small sacrifice. These nurses were downright giddy with delight. For the most part, I was totally preoccupied. Due, in part, to raging hormones and inborn neurosis, I felt my mood jerking from overwhelming astonishment—Cole's utter awesomeness was too much to take in—and hints of doom—either he was the most peaceful baby since Emmanuel himself or the child had stopped breathing. I was very confused.

In the distance, I heard a sister say, "Girl, you did your thing!" If she was happy I was happy. But I didn't see why she thought I had somehow exerted control and power over the age-old events of childbirth. Was it my uterine prowess or maybe the skillful conditioning and prep work of my vaginal walls that accounted for Cole's swift arrival?

All I did was do as that old, black woman at the bus stop had told me years prior—right before I had Chloe: "Let it do what it do." Still, these nurses were clearly into the whole thing. One of the nurses even joked, "You may as well go home!" The others laughed in agreement.

It was white noise as far as I was concerned. Mark, on the other hand, was loving it. In effect I was being heralded as the birthing game's MVP, which made (by extension) his seed and (by further extension) him the man of the hour.

I'd come to notice that after the birth of each of my kids, their dad enjoyed playing a key role. Not in my recovery or anything as dull as that. He'd get very excited in the play-by-play analysis. With about twenty-five minutes of pushing, Chloe took longest to arrive and made me work a little bit. Still, I wish I had a dollar for every time I heard Mark tell someone, "It was nothing. The baby just came right out!"

He won't admit it. But Trinity's entrance left him too shaken to say much of anything. But now with Cole, it was as though I were Mike Tyson and he was my Cus D'Amato. I would later learn that he was taking in every word of the nurses' sideline chatter.

I was too busy falling deeply in love. When Cole was born, I knew life could not get any better than that moment. To this day, I remember that awestruck feeling of swooning, nose-wide-open love and adoration. Once in a while, Cole still can make my heart skip a beat. I guess that's why he's my favorite child. But please don't tell anyone, because mothers are really not supposed to say such things.

To truly appreciate the miraculous beauty of Cole, you have to consider the boy's deft timing and attention to detail. This man-child was the truth! And it soon became clear to me, even then, that Cole was brought here to earth to make my life just a little bit easier. Think about it. He was thoughtful enough not to announce his arrival in the wee hours of the night. Where would we have found a sitter? Would we have had to wake the girls? He loved me enough not to plan an entrance in the middle of the day. Would I drive myself to the hospital? And who would meet the bus once the girls were let out of school? Cole also had keen insights and compassion. He knew that—while he was thoroughly loved and adored—his fretful mama was so busy being anxious that she hadn't put a single contingency plan in place in the event of an ill-timed burst of contractions. So my baby did what any strong man would do. He made things easy for me—a born leader, that boy.

On account of Cole's strategic planning and executive thinking, once the hospital staff stopped yammering long enough to get him properly cleaned, cleared, and checked into the nursery, it was almost noon. That gave Mark enough time to go drive back to Jersey, pick up the girls from school, and bring them to the hospital. Just as important, it also gave him time to get my dinner: a chicken Reuben sandwich, sweet potato fries, and malted milkshake—all of which I preordered, instructing the girls (in case their dad forgot) to handle the what-where-when of my first-meal wishes. Chloe and Trinity were instantly smitten when they met Cole.

It was obvious that Chloe, eight years his senior, had secretly dubbed herself Cole's "other mother." She held him with a kind of maternal authority. I could tell that Trinity, at six, was taken with his uncanny resemblance to the wrinkly Baby Alive doll stuffed in the toy chest. Yet there was a palpable bewilderment in her eyes. She stared at him for what seemed like hours, then looked up at me as though she'd been pondering the secrets of the universe: "Why is our baby so . . . um, white?" she asked.

"His color hasn't come in. That's all," I assured her; admittedly the old-school earlobe and cuticle check did not bode well for his browning prospects. "What matters most is what's on the inside. Right?" She nodded, with reservation. No doubt, my response was less than satisfactory. But I could tell she'd quickly decided to love him anyway. My Trinity has always been sweet like that.

All the excitement of the past twelve hours or so began to catch up with the girls. Their infatuation with Cole, the novelty of being in a fancy New York City building, and looking out onto the peaceful waters of the East River. They were ready to do what they normally do when we get together in the evening—cut up. How did a hospital bed work? What happens when you press this button or that one? Within minutes they'd invented all kinds of new games with the room-dividing curtain. Trinity—who is a one-kid variety show—was putting on a song and dance number. Chloe was trying to press the call buttons in the bathroom.

It suddenly dawned on me: This whole mother-of-three thing could possibly really suck. I've now got a whole mess of kids. As wonderful and beautiful and healthy and curious as children are, dealing with all their energy is going to wear my old butt out. My dismay could've been tied to the fact that in the hours since Cole's birth, my booty and all my nether regions had begun throbbing in pain. It wasn't constant or necessarily excruciating. But I was being reminded that a not-unsubstantial mass of flesh and bones had made its way out of me in fairly short order. The discomfort, which had been mostly on-again and then off-again, was now on-again. And it gave me pause.

I began thinking, maybe I should've had a long discussion with Mark at some point over the past ten months— explaining what might lie ahead and how we two would need to make some adjustments. I could've perhaps read up on growing your marriage and teamwork—perhaps done some bonding exercises or something, to prepare for this threesome inevitability. But, oh yeah . . . I never actually saw the inevitable. Did I? That acknowledgment brought me back to the practical matters at hand.

Mark would need to dash over to Route 3 for a serious Target run. Old King Cole needed *everything*, and he needed it now: diapers, onesies, hats, socks. I know you might be thinking, "Wait . . . Why would a springtime baby need hats and socks?" Good question. Us black people typically never let our babies outside without head-to-toe covering. My mama, her mama . . . it's just what we do. Then Mark would need to run all the newly bought items through the wash, double rinse cycle, and bring them back to the hospital—preferably in a fresh, new Glad storage bag. I bum-rushed him out of the hospital, secretly relieved that I had a legit reason for him and my loud squealing children to exit.

The next morning, after proudly performing his assigned duties, Mark rang me in the middle of my flavorless hospital breakfast just as I was jonesing for a cup of real coffee. Those who know me, even in passing, know that enduring the torture of sipping Folgers far exceeded that of contractions, back labor, or even the harrowing thought of an episiotomy. Mark was not calling so much to see how I was faring. In perfunctory fashion, he was checking in:

- The girls got off to school just fine.
- They were excited about the surprise gifts I left for them, especially the "I'm a Big Sister" T-shirts and candy cigars.

- My mom's flight was scheduled to arrive on time, and he'd pick her up from the airport in the afternoon.
- And, oh, should he come up to the room to help me with the baby or pull up to the hospital door and honk when he picked us up?

Okay, that last one is a source of debate between Mark and me—even after all these years. He could be right. Maybe he didn't "say it like *that*." But the fact remains: Less than twenty-four hours after a fully developed human being had relentlessly driven itself from my womb, crashed sacs and membranes, careened past my bladder and other sensitive organs, pushed through a wee-bitty tunnel, and hurtled out of my pelvis—he'd presumed I was good to go.

After all, that was yesterday. I'd had a good night's sleep. It was time to move on. Right?

As you might have gathered by now, I am a woman rarely without words. Let me say that this was one of them—a moment when my mouth opened up and no audible syllable could escape. After a few seconds, simply this: "I won't be leaving the hospital today." Very purposefully, each phonetic sound was articulated with careful, slow conviction. But that was lost on Mark, who said, ". . . No? Because the nurses said . . . So I just thought. You know . . ."

Do I laugh or cry, I wondered. I slurped the now-tepid brown water cruelly disguised as coffee while Mark began to repeat the nurses' praises. He was clearly under the impression that this talk somehow gassed up my head. So I listened for two or three minutes, then quietly sighed. "Let me let you go . . ." which is black-speak for "I'm tired of talking to you."

What I love most about New York Hospital is the view. I looked out across the East River wistfully. Having a baby always left me feeling this strange mix of joy and sadness—a subtle melancholy sets in after the euphoria of birthing life. And that comedown was starting to set in. This time, more than ever. Let's face it, there was no earthly reason a woman like me—well past childbearing age—should have been blessed with a healthy baby. I had friends in their midthirties still hoping for just one child; here I had three. Just like Mama.

And, oh snap, Mama's plane would soon land. More than twenty years after leaving home, I had to admit I still had some weird need to please the woman who'd raised me. For Mama, there was never any excuse for looking broke down. So I quickly showered and got myself together as best I could—considering that I hadn't packed so much as powder or lip gloss and was forced to rely on cheap hospital shampoo and conditioner.

But Cole, so named in honor of Mama's late mother's

maiden name, was the headliner here. When Mark brought her to the hospital and Mama saw her first grandson, she was brought to tears. To my mind, Cole looked like a little old man—an incredibly beautiful little old man, mind you, but a little old man just the same. Mama saw Papa—her father—in the shape of Cole's head, in his eyes, and—as she struggled to explain—in his spirit. Heaven only knows the complex web of emotions those memories brought to the surface. She held that boy like he was the precious Baby Jesus—barely taking her eyes off his.

That is, unless you count the instant her gaze took hold of me and she felt moved to comment on my thick waist. "From the looks of your stomach, it looks like they left Cole's brother or sister up in there." She laughed. "Are you sure you're not pregnant again already?"

She smirked toward Mark, who for once had the good sense not to laugh. More than likely, he didn't even hear her. Slumped over in the visitor's chair staring absent-mindedly out the window, Mark was very tired. You see, the traffic had really wiped him out. After a hearty laugh—solo—Mama soon moved past my baby weight gain. She and Mark passed Cole back and forth. If either of them wondered whether I was hungry or thirsty, they did not let on. They left an hour or so later and I enjoyed a tasty hospital meal of chicken and something posing as mashed potatoes. Hmm-hmm.

There was no sense being all sensitive, I reasoned. A postpartum sister needed to rest up. I'd be discharged the next day and I'd need all my strength to attend the girls' school talent show that evening. Deep down, though, I think I knew that all the sleep in the world is no help to a sister who is sick and tired.

Now, given our past, you might assume that the postnatal, prickly dynamic between Mama and me might've softened a bit. And you'd be right, sorta-kinda. In our typical family fashion, we'd really never talked about the discord. Was it a battle of wills? Some petty jealousies? Some spillover resentments? Or all of the above. We'd never know.

What I did know was that during her stay, Mama worked in the garden as though she were a hired field hand. I was staying out of her way. I'd leave the house for little errands—to buy breast pump supplies or nursing pads—and try to align my returns to Cole's feedings. Remember, "busy" was like Mama's secret government name. Each day, when she wasn't spending untold hours weeding and trimming the hydrangeas (and heaven knows what else grew out there), she was chastising Mark and me about weeding and pruning. It was a "thing." Not just the backyard, really, but the front hedges, the driveway, the sidewalk—the house, in general. In the years since we'd become suburbanites, she'd harped on the house's outward appearance most every visit. In the fall, we failed to rake the leaves often enough. In the spring, our grass was not green enough. These were all mostly Mark's fault. But I shared equal blame. I could've at least swept the walkway regularly and cleaned the storm door—the right way, with vinegar, not Windex, of course. Mind you, this is someone who insisted her three kids scour oil stains off the garage floor.

I tried to simply brush off Mama's litany of criticisms. She was, after all, getting on in years. If she got her rocks off by digging in dirt—and taking digs at me—so be it. It's just that on this particular visit, I really needed the nagging to stop. My hormones had not quite settled. And when Cole was discharged, the doctor was concerned about his jaundice levels.

During our first week at home, I had to take him to the hospital each day, where they'd draw blood from his tiny feet and make him cry. On several of these occasions, Mama instructed me to "run by Home Depot" on my way back and pick up a bag of mulch. I pretended not to hear her—hoping she would take the hint. She did not.

On the third or fourth day of my regular trips to the local hospital, where my newborn child was being stabbed before my eyes, Mama brought up the mulch thing once again. I know there are adults—even kids, for goodness' sake—who think nothing of cursing at, or in front of, their parents. Generally speaking (and by now, I'm sure you've noticed that I am full of generalizations), black people don't play that. It's like wearing shorts in sixty-degree weather. We just don't.

That being said, I have to admit that this here black person was perilously close to cussing her mama OUT. If her mulch fixation were not enough, she'd even devised a plan to heave the hefty wood chips into the car without straining my still-raw innards.

"All you have to do . . ." Mama began. I put up my hand, mostly as a means to calm my own self. She would later claim that I "gave her the hand," a gross misinterpretation. I tried to say nicely that I had no intention of taking my newborn into Home Depot—a veritable cesspool filled with the germs of sweaty, unbathed landscapers, contractors, and whatnot. I might've left it at that. But I just couldn't. I added, admittedly with some disdain, that on my list of priorities the backyard was hovering at number 437.

I left in a huff. When I returned, this time a tad earlier than Cole's scheduled nursing time, Mama didn't hear me walk into the house. But I heard her. She was on the phone with my sister. "Oh, it's that bad, all right. You would have to see this mess to believe it. And this little heifer takes the cake. I know good and well she hears me talking and she walks around here like she's deaf and dumb. . . ."

I quietly crept up the stairs. For no particular reason I took Cole out of his bassinet and laid him on the bed next to me. Mama always says, "Don't disturb a sleeping baby." To hell with that.

CHAPTER NINE

Three the Hard Way

Way back in the days when Mark and I were dating, we talked about having a family in that cute way stupid, lovesick couples do—using TV households like the Huxtables as guides. He said he wanted two kids. I said I'd hoped we'd have three. He squashed that—with what, at the time, seemed sound reasoning. He delivered a sports analogy, which I didn't entirely understand but struck me as well thought out: Two kids with two parents, he said, was simple man-on-man defense. But with three, you've gotta switch to zone.

We hadn't been dating very long. Who knew whether we'd remain a couple—let alone marry and have children. I nodded and probably feigned agreement with something like, "Yeeeah, zone . . . I know what you mean." I did get it, sort of. This was back in the nineties when Patrick Ewing and the Knicks actually made the playoffs pretty regularly. In truth, I don't know a pick 'n' roll from a sushi roll. But I did enjoy watching tall, muscular men run across my living room screen now and again.

The play-by-play commentary by the Knicks broadcaster, Walt "Clyde" Frazier, packed in as many laughs as an *SNL* skit could hope for (this was the very unfunny David Spade era). He'd split infinitives, mix metaphors, and try to showcase his vocabulary skills with phrases like, "Miller displays tremendous tenacity to go along with his sagacity," "What a provocative pass!" and "The Pistons are off to a prolific start!" His erudite observations were not limited to the game. When the camera panned attractive women in the stands, he might offer commentary as well—for example, "I like my women bodacious, not loquacious." The Knicks-legend-turned-broadcaster, with his penchant for Mac Daddy suits and busting rhymes, was (and still is) wildly entertaining. He took his role seriously and tried to teach viewers all about "posting and toasting" and "shaking and baking," as well as "swishing and dishing." I'm not quite old enough—or sports-savvy enough—to fully appreciate his championship-worthy basketball skills. But for the genius of his legendary lexicon, in my book he is a pimp-suited, bombastic Hall of Famer.

Pity I didn't listen. I mean *really, really* listen to Clyde. There were nuances to his play-by-play account of defense

that I just missed. I thought he was just styling and profil-
ing. When he used words like *prescient*, *altruistic*, and *intuit*
to describe a defensive play, I was busy giggling at the
man's use (and sometimes abuse) of the English language
when I should've been taking notes.

Now here I am with Mark, backcourt in the unlikeliest
of positions. Three kids. I don't have Tenacious D, or any
other pithy Clyde-like types of D. What's even worse is I
failed to put two and two together back when Mark came
up with his analogy on family planning. You know how it
is when you start dating someone. You're not always thinking clearly. My point is, although he has many fine qualities
(responsible, hardworking), Mark is not—and has never
been—a baller or shot caller. He went to college on a *football* scholarship. On the hardwood, I don't think dude's
skills are all that. I would even venture to say, he gots no
game. It's not his fault. His body is somewhat top-heavy—
all torso, short legs. Such genetics are great for tackling.
Jump shot? Layups? Uh-uh.

The point is this: I had myself a *sich-e-ation*. Not to be
confused with a situation—an ordinary, run-of-the-mill
problem. A situation is merely challenging. The kind of
thing that can usually find a simple fix. This thing I'm
talking about? Not so much. A *sich-e-ation* means TROU-
BLE with a capital *T*. Let me break it down.

I don't pretend to know the *X*'s and *O*'s of B-balling

strategy but what I do know—thanks to Clyde—boils down to this: Zone defense takes coordinating, which explains Mark's preference for man-to-man. See, he is not exactly a collabo type of guy. In zone play, from what I gather, the teammates talk to one another a lot and make snap moves and adjustments. They quickly gel. They play off one another.

Do I have to draw you a picture or can you see where I'm going with this? Mama had an expression for reticent folks like Mark. She'd say, "You know so-and-so wouldn't say *shit* if he had a mouth full of it." Crude, for sure, but that about sums things up. I had to learn the hard way that players who are tight-lipped and short-legged don't make for the best zone defenders. I say all this to say that once we went from two kids to three, in the day-to-day rhythms of things I was basically on my own. In the paint.

I don't regret having a third child. I know I'm blessed. But—especially in the wake of those first several months— I began to feel the meaning of a phrase Mama used often. Her most dire warning ended with a nonsensical reference to "shit creek" and how one might be stranded on this eminent body of water with no paddle. As a child, I always wondered to myself, "Why on earth does she have to call it 'shit creek'? Wouldn't any creek be pretty treacherous without a means to row?"

It all made sense once baby number three arrived. I

was in deep doo-doo. And I knew not what to do. Overwhelmed is what a mother feels with one or two little kids. This third took things to a new level. It was shock and awe, just like George W said our troops were going to lay on Saddam Hussein. Do you happen to know the militaristic definition of such a strategy? It's known as rapid dominance. That's what was happening up in my house.

The girls, still little, were not accustomed to sharing me. So I felt the need to overcompensate to make sure they didn't feel slighted. Their activities—Brownies, soccer, swimming—didn't stop with the birth of the new baby. Had I managed to wrap my head around the idea that the basketball-sized bulge I'd been toting around for the better part of the year was a human being that would actually be born, I'd have pared things down considerably. But I'd seen pregnancy the movie before and it did not end in "happily ever after."

Call it neurotic. Call it denial. Call it what you like. I just felt, in my heart, that it was probably not a good idea to get too fixed on an outcome. This final scene could feature a real live baby. Or . . . not. I have a dear old friend who is super-analytical and thoughtful and goal oriented. I'll call her Andrea—mainly because that's her name and also because I'm not telling tales out of school. She knows this about herself. We've never discussed it, but I am sure she dreams in Excel. I'm not mad because it works for her.

I think Andrea gets her hair cut every three weeks—to the day. Her teeth are cleaned regularly and her doctor visits are plotted out on a quarterly basis. As for me? A Pap smear definitely occurred at some point during Obama's first term. When exactly? I'm not sure.

As the pregnancy progressed she'd ask me things like, "What's your plan for having three kids?" "Have you thought about how you will prioritize your time?" "If you were a tree, what kind of tree would you be?" Okay, I made up that last one. My point is, I consider myself a relatively prudent person. I plan summer camp schedules, biannual wardrobe purges, and holiday dinners. Although it rarely happens, I take great pride in planning my grocery shopping—replete with lists, coupons, and bonus-buy cards actually on my person, not in the sofa cushions or the other purse. I've successfully planned for retirement—contingent upon a few lifestyle adjustments such as acquiring a taste for Spam, dried beans, and Vienna sausages.

Granted, I could've gone out to buy a changing pad, and maybe a few nursing bottles would've been nice to have on hand. BabyCenter probably has a flow chart template or something for "introducing" a third child into the mix. But really there is no way to plan—sight unseen—for another living creature to roll up in your already precarious maternal core and take up permanent residence.

I came home from the hospital with Cole on a Friday afternoon. That evening I dragged myself to the girls' talent show. The next day, functioning on about three hours' sleep, I woke up to an arsenal of hair gel, combs, barrettes, and elastic ties so they'd be picture-perfect for their afternoon piano recitals. No small feat—as both Chloe and Trinity have more hair than Samson and all his Nazirite brethren combined. Nowhere in the Bible is there any mention of Ultra Sheen or Frizz-Ease, for that matter, but I am convinced that there had to have been some special holy elixir stylists used to tame lamb's-wool kinks. I've prayed for revelation to no avail so far. At any rate, girls are sensitive creatures; I had to help them get their pretty on each day and try to remain cheerful and engaged— with or without a newborn tethered to my body and literally sucking the life out of me every two hours.

My girls knew I was not quite myself. Probably my crying jags, bouts of narcolepsy, and not-infrequent cussing tipped them off. They are as smart as they are beautiful—which is saying a lot. I reminded them often that my moodiness had nothing to do with them. Rather sleep deprivation was making Mama batty. I told them so often that Trinity took it upon herself to act as my emissary when folks called the house. As I lay on the sofa one day— nodding off as she and her sister did their homework—I overheard her answer the phone and, in her most authoritative kindergartner parlance, explain to my sister:

"Auntie, Mom can't come to the phone right now. She is cranky and tired—but not on purpose. It's on account of baby brother. When we go to sleeping and dream, Mommy only shuts her eyes for a little, teensy bit of sleep. Then she wakes back up to feed Cole. Then she rests for another couple of minutes and wakes up again. She has to do this about four million times. Then morning comes and she has to get up—even if really she wants to stay in bed for longer."

Mark had mysteriously forgotten much about newborns—despite past experience. Specifically, he failed to recall the nature of babies' sleep needs—and, more specific (and important), he didn't remember *my* sleep needs. During the first few weeks of Cole's life, I'd bring the baby into our bed for feedings. Instead of getting up to help, drowsy-eyed Mark would turn to gaze lovingly at his son and then roll over and go back to sleep. Once, when my sleep deprivation and anger had given way to a rare moment of lucid thinking, I asked, "When are you planning to join the late-night party? You do realize there is pumped milk in the fridge." Mark stared me in the eye, all befuddled and whatnot: "Oh, I don't know. I hadn't thought about that."

I didn't go off in that moment, but perhaps I should've. I held in the rage and calmly explained, as though this were our first child, how important it was that I get more sleep—for my health, sanity, and milk production—not to mention the added bonus of staving off homicidal urges. So much for restraint, self-control, and all that mature stuff. I snapped just a few days later. I was behind on a story deadline, and when Mark came home from work I described how crazy the day had been—trying to interview folks and write between Cole's erratic naps. I thought he was hearing me. We'd been trying to put off daycare or outside help until Cole got a little older. But it was clear that if I was going to take on even small assignments, the childcare issue needed solving—quickly.

It just so happens that during this same period, repairmen were working on our roof. Actually, they were fixing only a part of the roof. It was not a huge job. They came in the mornings and left by late afternoon. The day after I'd meticulously laid out all the reasons why writing articles around a newborn's schedule was untenable, Mark came home from work a tad early. The roofers had not yet finished up. He casually grabbed something to drink from the refrigerator. Then he looked at me and said, "Were you able to get any writing done with all the loud noise the workers are making?"

That's when I lost it.

Really? I am bathing, suckling, burping, changing, and caring for a tiny creature that sleeps in two-to-three-hour intervals. And you think workers pounding on the roof are my greatest life disruption?

Mama was trying to be helpful—in her way. Not that she cooked and froze meals or anything. I mean helpful in the sense that her more-than-ample output of advice was now ratcheted up to high gear. She called often with gentle reminders.

- I should sleep when Cole slept—even with a six- and eight-year-old in my care.
- I should have Mark clean the garage, so the kids could play in there safely.
- I should have Mark weed the yard, because she spotted some poison ivy back there.
- I should be sure to massage the baby so he'd sleep better at night—like that was going to buy me five extra hours.
- And, of course, I should "give that baby some formula, for God's sake!"

CHAPTER TEN

Talking Loud and Saying Nothing

Like suffrage, equal pay, and leak-free feminine protection, the comfort of sister friends is a basic, inalienable Woman's Right. Think about it. We are, by our very nature, the connected gender; we need interaction. And talking is good. Certainly, moms need affirmation, validation, support. Generally, I have a lot to say—about most everything.

And I thought, maybe—just maybe—I should do what millions of other moms do when they are starved for human interaction with like-minded folk. But something about the whole group thing just felt wrong. Probably, I thought, the whole get-together idea is another one of those things that work in theory. Like those fat-fighting fitness trainers who tell us all to taste just a bite of brownie to sate a sweet tooth. Yeah, that makes sense and all. But who would do that? Some kind of freak?

That's exactly what I feel like up in this piece tonight. A big ole freak. Apparently this is what folks do in the sub-urbs. I tell you what: This here life of single-family-home-owning, no-car-alarm-blaring, grass-mowing, cricket-chirping, neighbor-chatting, school-bus-stop-waiting, potluck-dinner-hosting, and big-box-grocery-shopping was more than a notion. Who knew just a simple move across a river could turn a sister's life upside down? Maybe it's time I stop fighting this bedroom community and go with the flow. From a cursory look around the joint, you might think I was in a Shonda Rhimes drama of some kind. Just about every race and creed is represented. This town is so diverse! Everyone here likes to say that, brag about it, pat their liberal backs with it. No matter who you ask, gay, lesbian, white, black, yellow, and green people alike will say, "We chose this town for its diversity." Then they just kind of beam at themselves with self-satisfaction like they deserve a cookie.

Truth is, the town is not all that diverse. It is mostly a Crayola-box mix of left-leaning races and ethnicities gath-ered up together in one place. I'm not going to lie, I was smitten with this place once I learned its population was 30 percent black. I wasn't trying to have my kids be the only beans up in the Uncle Ben's. Like many, I fell for the okey-doke. Don't get me wrong. It's not as though this is not a lovely place to live. But how diverse can a place be if the average home costs well over a half million dollars. (Not mine. I said *average*. As usual, I be pulling up the rear.) My point is that a kettle full of affluent people—who happen to be green, white, black, brown, and yellow—do not a melting pot make.

People here have rich folks' problems—not the kind of inconveniences most of America would call, you know, problematic problems. As in causing a threat to their daily existence. Where I'm from, a real problem means you don't have gas money. You're at the cash register and you have to put things back—things you actually need. Bill collectors call your house. Out here, people's problems are in their heads, for the most part. There is this pressure and that pressure—social stuff, really.

And these nonproblems apparently afflict all races in my town. I have white friends who tell me they're jealous of their nannies. I have black friends who tell me their cleaning ladies half step. And nearly every mother you meet worries like a mug. About their kid's self-esteem. About their kid's social skills. About their kid's scores on the statewide assessment tests. Testing concerns are big in these parts. I don't love the fact that school districts want to test your kids to within an inch of their lives either. But I be like, "You want me to sign how many petitions and come to how many Monday night Board of Ed meetings?"

This is going to sound racist (I'm sorry, I can't help it).

But growing up, I thought only white people acted so . . . I don't know. What's the word? *Whack.* But I stand corrected. I met a black mother who, in great frenetic detail, explained the vexing situation posed by having her sitter travel to Martha's Vineyard with the family to mind her two children. She somehow believed I'd be able to relate to her quandary. She reasoned that the sitter should be paid less than her normal fee, because after all the woman would have the privilege of caring for her trifling rugrats by the sea. Are you following? She was doing the sitter a favor—giving her a perk. Perhaps the caregiver shouldn't be paid at all to wipe snotty noses and chase after Bebe's kids since she was getting a free trip out of the deal. Another black woman I knew casually once tried to engage me in a serious conversation about body makeup. You see, her knees were very dark, she explained. She planned to wear a short dress, with no panty hose, to an upcoming charity event and wanted my thoughts on which shade she should apply to her legs—Caramel Honey or Butter Pecan. Trust, you can't make this stuff up!

For all of its diversity—real or imagined—a suburb is a suburb, when you break it on down. I get it, I suppose. I've seen what happens on Wisteria Lane. Women in this kind of environment start to go batty after a while. It's tough, no doubt, to sit trapped inside your own heady self-importance. They need to get out. That's what I thought I was doing by coming here, but I should've followed my first mind and got myself a pint of ice cream—which I was doing a lot of lately.

I'm here now. So what's done is done. I tried to think cool, "I-got-this" thoughts. Not easy. As I stooped to sit and caught a glimpse of my flabby thighs, jiggling like placenta, one of life's truths revealed its ugly self: Seems that even while clad in pricey premium jeans, doughy postpartum flesh is prone to bust out like a can of cheap biscuits banged across the counter.

The whole notion of stepping out like this went against everything I was taught. Mama always warned against this kind of thing. She's always been a girlfriend's girlfriend. However, she had serious misgivings about surrounding herself with a whole gaggle of women. But, alas, Mama ain't here. And desperate times call for—well, you know. So I sat. Apparently, I was supposed to shed all my inhibitions and just let go. That's what I'd been told. Fortunately, there was wine. *Lots* of wine.

I was ready. I'd mapped out my game plan, opting for a coy-earnest combo of my own invention. A neat trick that mimicked the back-and-forth of a lively conversation but, at the same time, required virtually no speaking on my part. It worked like this: Random person says "Hello." I *could* say "Hi" back and extend my hand for a shake. Doing so, however, creates an opening—albeit small—that says:

"Hey, I am interested in you and what you have to say."
That's not the vibe I'm going for tonight. So it's important
to ditch the verbal greeting. Instead I make eye contact,
with arched brows, and smile sweetly—not a toothy grin,
just upturned mouth. You have to know me to understand
that this takes supreme effort. I like smiling. I like laughing. And usually, I get a kick out of meeting new people.
But I need to be careful; I don't know what I'm getting
myself into here.

If dialogue begins to build, I still sit mute. Occasionally
I tilt my head in puppylike wonder. Other times I just sort
of nod—carefully furrowing my brow for high-serious effect. Think Ann Curry, the old *Today* anchor, as she'd shift
from a feel-good segment to a broiling world crisis. Not to
brag or anything, but I am *working* it. I can't get over my
sheer brilliance. Sure, I'm a bit dizzy for all the tilting,
nodding, and furrowing. But it's totally worth it. I can literally feel my own swagger. I am coming off engaged,
thoughtful, and maybe a tad mysterious. Mama's got it
going on . . . that is, until, all kinds of crazy breaks loose.

It happened with lightning-quick speed. First, the dis-
tinct sound of weeping. Quite naturally, as the mother of
small kids, I ignore it. Then as the wails start to escalate, so
does my agitation. *Really? Tears? No one told me there would
be crying up in here.* I'm talking shakes, snotty-nosed blath-

ering. The whole nine. Between the sobs, spliced sound bites flow. I struggle to decipher the words, which break up like bad cell phone reception: "Bad" or "sad" mother; "nipples," possibly "ripples," and over and over again with the pounding indignation of an exorcist at work came shrieks of "sucking" and "sucking" and "sucking." Or maybe it was a word that rhymes with *sucking*. I hope not, because while I'm no prude, I don't get down like that in public.

Turns out, that first outburst was simply the overture. Within moments, a gaggle of women launch into a pitiful philharmonic. Amid the cries, I hear words like *lonely*, *confused*, *overwhelmed*, and *sexless*. Then, just as I am struggling to pierce the confusion, three words blare out loud and clear: "Nobody *understands* me!"

That's when it hit me. GAWD! I *HATE* MOMMY GROUPS!

There. I said it. I'm sorry. Well, actually I'm not. Mommy Groups are supposedly designed to support mothers—an honorable notion. But in practice I think Mommy Groups are counterproductive. The roundtable talkfest about every ounce of baby minutiae does not bolster a mother's confidence; it dilutes it. By subjecting every ounce of a natural maternal thought to CT scan–like scrutiny, the whole Mommy Group thing can suck the life—and light—out of any mother. The tragic truth is:

Mommy Groups mark the beginning of the end of common sense. I heard a mother self-diagnose her six-year-old son with "oppositional defiance" (a fancy term for when your kid won't mind you) because he "has a will of his own." That set off a wave of "I think my kid has that too" and "I know a good therapist . . ."

Clearly, these chicks and I just don't click. Aside from ovaries, we have nothing in common, which I knew— sorta, kinda—I suppose. But this—a night when 7 For All Mankind proves to be anything but kind to thighs like mine—pretty much confirms it. If nothing else, my Bobbi Brown illuminating finish powder has lived up to its name. I have seen the light. And it's high time I face facts: I am a misfit mom. Lord knows I've tried. But I don't belong here. On a purely practical level, it can be a sometimes-struggle to even sustain a conversation with some of these women. I'm a freelance writer now. I don't commute into the city every day to a nine-to-five. And although I am at home throughout the day, I'm not a stay-at-home mom in the classic sense. Deadlines call. I can't always post up at Starbucks weekday mornings.

More important, this obsession with home and hearth bores me. I mean, I love my kids as much as the next mom. I just don't want to sit around talking about them all the time. Don't get it twisted; it's not like I'm all that.

Trust me. I sucked at breast-feeding. Chloe never did

latch according to the La Leche (make that "la leeches") method. And once, when I accidentally clipped Trinity's nails *and* her sweet little fingertips, I wailed louder than she did. I obsessed for days—calling everyone I knew to talk me off the cliff. Don't even get me started on those dark days when—with a two-week-old, a two-year-old, a new house, a new town (in New Jersey, no less, which may as well be a new country), and a new job—I danced on the edge of despair for a solid year. Guess what? It passed. Soon after, of course, some new anguish set in. I certainly had no plans to become pregnant with a third child in my forties. But where would I be without Cole, the Bonus Baby?

Long story short: The world is full of confusion, upset, drama, and darkness. It's called life, boo.

CHAPTER ELEVEN

Don't Let the Mother-Suckers Get You Down

Mama always said that there was no bigger fool than an educated fool. I paid her no mind. I didn't think the line even made sense, because if you were educated, how could you be a fool? Right? I have reached that point in my life. We don't have to call it middle age. Let's call it half-time. At any rate, I'm there—at that stage where I can't help but look over my past. And like Arsenio Hall used to say: "Some of the things make you go, 'Hmmmm.'"

Somewhere in my idyllic view of life with a nice family, a nice life, I pictured myself being happy. At the very least approaching a modicum of contentment. Instead, most every day I feel like I'm not enough of this, too much of that. More often than I'd care to admit, I take myself back to those long-ago days growing up with Mama when life was simple. She was so matter-of-fact about everything. Her words often wounded, but I guess that's why they say the truth hurts. She'd tell us kids things like, "In the end, the only person you can truly count on is you, so be true to you."

I suppose that's why I am beginning to chafe over this idea of modern motherhood. There was apparently a memo that went out to the world at large. And in it, there were new parenting guidelines laid down. Rules dictating that all of us with kids were to forfeit our lives—our souls, even—to the single-minded pursuit of child rearing. 24/7. Without ceasing. This role, it seems to have been written, should govern our every thought and supersede all prior conventions of sound judgment, discernment, and plain old motherwit.

Not long after Cole transitioned to his big-boy bed— allegedly—I ran into an old friend. I'd known Sandy for more than twenty years. Her background is very similar to mine: modest upbringing, blue-collar parents, first-generation professional. Imagine how excited I was to discover a "for-real sister" in the midst of all the desperate housewives I was meeting in my newly adopted suburban town. We reconnected as mothers and inevitably the subject of kids and sleep—or in her case, lack thereof—came up. I told her I had let my baby "work it out" when he cried in the middle of the night. Girlfriend looked me dead in the eye and said, "Aren't you worried you'll create abandonment issues?" I thought she was kidding. So I burst out laughing. Quickly I realized she could be serious, and through nervous giggles I asked incredulously, "You think a two-minute crying jag is gonna scar my kid?" And she responded as though my actions were worthy of a Child and Family Services intervention: "I'm just such a mom, I couldn't imagine making my baby cry."

I thought to myself, "Now, ain't that a mother-sucker!"

Surely, it's happened to you too. No woman with a child is immune from this sort of stealth HateHer-Ade. I once had the same thing happen to me years prior. I showed up at a kiddie party looking especially cute—if I do say so myself (it doesn't happen often). People act funny when a mother looks good, even when it is a rare event. Maybe they suspect that your self-sacrificing, self-flagellating, and abject-selflessness game is shaky if you don't look like something the cat dragged in. Or maybe it's like Puff said on that collabo with Mace and B.I.G.—"*D to the A to the D-D-Y . . . Know you rather see me die than to see me fly . . .*" Mothers be hatin.'

It was early in the summer and I'd bought myself a brand-new pair of pink skinny jeans—colored denim was just coming out—and a tank top. It was white with flowers and the whole outfit was a fresh-to-def splurge. Another mom, one I barely knew, complimented me. And, Chatty Cathy that I am at times, l told her I had decided to treat myself. That mother-sucker—who, might I add, looked as though she was wearing the clothes she slept in, said to me: "Oh, I never buy nice things for myself now that I'm a mom!"

See what I'm saying? Some people think I have an attitude. I don't say this proudly. It's just one of those things—like flat feet and thick thighs—I've come to accept about myself. At this point, you may have picked up a bit of a bad-ass vibe from me. So I can totally see why you may be waiting for me to tell you I slammed that heifer but good. You may even be salivating right now wondering what kind of in-your-face comeback I spat at the tired mother-sucking woman who had the nerve to question my motherhood.

If you are hearing crickets, it's not just you. I hate to let you down. But I'm not so different from you. Of course, when I walked *away* from the scene, I read that shrew like a waiting room copy of *In Touch* magazine. But right then, right there? I was speechless. I mean what do you expect? Like Sandy, she blindsided me, as classic mother-suckers are wont to do. First I was hit with the whole Dr. Phil–like, psychobabble abandonment thing—which, for a hot minute, I considered even though I knew deep down that it was all kinds of crazy. Then, before I could barely recover, the judgment jab came flying at me—only bad mothers let their babies cry, after all. Real moms don't buy themselves anything.

So, alas, I am partly to blame. I know I shouldn't have

let them win. None of us *want* these no-gooders to get away with such heinous acts. It's just that few of us realize how much is at stake. We have no idea we are in the fight of our lives. We don't even know the mother-suckers are winning. And *that's* the rub. The perpetrator is very patient, working slowly and deliberately over time. More importantly, the classic mother-sucker operates on the down low, rarely out in the open.

You may be wondering: *If I can't actually see a mother-sucker, how will I know when I'm truly sucked?* That's a good question. The truth is: If you have children and you live anywhere in the Western Hemisphere, you're already sucked. The mother-suckers pretty much had you at "hello." And if you regularly frequent Mommy Groups and such, you're double sucked; they will squeeze the common sense out of a right-thinking mom.

Let me help you understand. Merriam-Webster has not gotten around to defining *mother-sucker* just yet, so I've taken the liberty to jump in:

moth • er–suck • er *n.*
muth' ur suk' ur

1. one who impairs, derails, countermines, or otherwise screws up Mama's groove
2. a despicable, sly person or situation that attempts to

play you like a dime-store harmonica, rendering said
   mother (common) senseless

3. any and all high-priced products and services that
   consist of invented crap no one really needs, or that
   promise to perfect a process that nature has done all
   by its damn self since the beginning of time

By now you have probably aptly concluded that Polly-
anna and I are not what you would call homegirls. I like to
speak real plain. I loathe confusion and ambiguity. For
many years now I have been a student of that great phi-
losopher from Detroit: Aretha Franklin. She may or may
not have been thinking about mother-suckers when she
blasted: "Let's call this thing *exactly* what it is!" Still, I lean
on her immortal words whenever I suspect a mother-
sucker is at work.

I cannot prove the undermining effect of the message.
I don't have definitive data to dispute the absurdity of it
all. But thanks to the Queen of Soul, I don't have to—and
neither do you. All you have to know is this: If "it's a funky
and low-down feeling . . ." rest assured, that's a mother-
sucker.

It has taken me way too long to see mother-suckers for
the destructive forces that they are. If you let them, they
will not only tear down your confidence. They will also

leave you racked with guilt at every turn—and worse, make you feel as worthless as a penny with a hole in it.

Nowadays it's open season on mothering. Everybody's a critic. Everybody is an expert on raising other people's kids. How can we explain the hot mess that is mommy-hood these days? *New York* magazine tried in "All Joy and No Fun," a much-talked-about cover story. In stark detail the author laid bare the mother-sucking truth. Many moms are left empty and disillusioned by the pressure to mold their little ones into perfect little creatures.

Let's face it. Scripting your every word to make sure you are talking so your kids will listen and listening so your kids will talk is tiring. Constantly working to boost your baby's brain power is a sure way to deplete your own. And studying the five habits of happy families makes every day feel like you are living in daily prep for the College Board exams. Does that sound like fun?

The writer quotes many hard statistics, some of which are of the "duh" variety that make one wonder who the heck pays these researchers to study the obvious and why. For example: Moms today report having less leisure time than their 1970s-era counterparts. That's a no-brainer. I'm not saying my mother didn't work hard to raise us. But I can clearly recall that on most days, my sibs and I were outside from sunup to sundown—leaving Mama scads of uninterrupted hours to smoke long cigarettes and watch Erica Kane scandalize Pine Valley. Fast-forward twenty-five years or so; I can remember that when my firstborn was old enough to scoot about, my mother was stunned to learn that we didn't stick her in a playpen. I looked at her in disbelief, as though she'd just suggested that I lock the kid in a closet. Horrors! Like other new moms I knew, I was playing or reading with my baby just about every waking moment of the day.

So it was no surprise to me that this study went on to reveal that 71 percent of mothers crave more time for themselves. But here's the kick in the head—from a mother-sucking point of view, that is: Despite the paucity of free time, a startling 85 percent of parents lament that they don't spend enough time with their children. If that's not crazy I don't know what is.

I call it a mother-sucking shame. What those numbers tell me is that how-to books, magazine articles, and sound bites have supplanted our innate ability to nurture, to love—in fact, to just *be*. Mothering is part of our natural identity. Whether one chooses to bear children or not, mothering is a part of us. And it's been snatched.

Ever see the movie *Malcolm X*, with Denzel Washington? Forget *Training Day*, for which he won an Academy Award. Anyone who truly loves and appreciates His Fineness can trace the actor's genius to this Spike Lee–directed biopic of 1992, where Denzel doesn't just portray Malcolm X, he *is* the slain civil rights hero. There is one powerful scene where Denzel stands among peeps on a crowded Harlem street, trying to explain the race problem in the United States. It's not so much the lack of jobs or the drug- and crime-ridden inner cities, he theorizes. No, it goes deeper than that. With a burning intensity in his eyes and his signature pouted lips (don't act like you haven't noticed that thing he does with his mouth), he declares: "We've been had. We've been took. We've been hoodwinked. Bamboozled. Led astray."

Mother-suckers have done that to a generation of moms. They are hardly new, not some newly discovered affliction. It's important to understand that the systematic erosion of a mother's confidence started way back in the day—not the nostalgic 1990s. Around the dawn of the twentieth century, a few pompous men decided moms needed teaching; they winnowed the art of maternal sway down to a daily script of rigor, charts, and schedules, leaving mothers feeling anxious and defeated as early as 1894. That's when Luther Emmett Holt's *The Care and Feeding of Children* ordered strict feeding times and potty training in the first year. Holt spent his time concocting complex alterations of cow's milk to mimic breast milk—in other words, formula—and his pediatric practice boasted such celeb patients as John D. Rockefeller.

By the 1920s, the field of social science began to grow, giving credence to Freudian ideas of child development. Holt's treatise was joined by John Watson's *Psychological Care of Infant and Child*, calling for even more dogma and dire warnings against hugs and kisses. "Mothers just don't know," he wrote. "When they kiss their children and pick them up . . . they are slowly building up a human being totally unable to cope with the world it must later live in."

Watson was probably the first prominent author to assert the most pervasive, and damning, themes of so-called expert parenting advice. And it's no coincidence that these mother-sucking ideas persist even today. In essence, Watson's almost hundred-year-old manual is predicated on two primary theories:

1. Mothering requires trained instruction. And physicians and psychologists—in fact, every Tom, Dick, and Tyrone—know better than Mom herself what's best for baby.
2. Children are more clay than complex creatures. Decisions like co-sleeping, breast-feeding, and time-outs are, therefore, the ultimate determinant to their success or failure.

Perhaps it was a blessing for motherhood that calamities like the Great Depression and World War II kept these notions from taking root in their psyches during the early days of the twentieth century. But the Expert Age of parenting was slowly building. Not coincidentally, the slow but steady erosion of good sense was increasingly problematic. A much lower-grade Mommy Mania even prompted Dr. Benjamin Spock to write in 1945:

> Don't take too seriously all that the neighbors say. Don't be overawed by what the experts say. Don't be afraid to trust your own common sense. Bringing up your child won't be a complicated job if you take it easy . . . what good mothers and fathers instinctively feel like doing for their babies is usually best after all . . .

If he were around today, I'm sure he would break it down just like I'm doing today. He was talking all gentle like, because things were not as bad then as they are now. And he probably didn't want to hurt anyone's feelings. Allow me to paraphrase: The old guy was trying to say: Don't let the mother-suckers get you down.

CHAPTER TWELVE

Feeling Froggy?

It was dinnertime circa 1977. I can't remember exactly what we were drinking. Most likely Kool-Aid, because why on earth would we be drinking anything other than the official beverage of black folks?

It was just-made. It was red. And it was sweet, just like I like it. But it was warm. Mama suggested I add ice. You know, to make the drink colder. I gave this some thought for a few moments. Then, I reasoned that Mama's advice was off base. "No, Mama," I'd said. "The ice will not cool the drink. The drink will warm the ice."

At first, she laughed. I was an aggravating kid—so much so that at times I guess my obnoxiousness took comical turns. Each of my own kids has inherited some of my grating tendencies. But there are nice words for it today— inquisitive or, perhaps, a critical thinker. But as far as Mama was concerned I was nothing as fancy as that. I was simply a pain. A smartass. I had an abundance of questions—and answers—to everything. And my queries and assertions were nearly always diametrically opposed to Mama's way of thinking. Meals were tough because my inner Ruth Reichl drove me to openly critique every dish served. I didn't realize that Mama was not just stretching her dollars to feed us, she was pulling dead presidents so tight George Washington's waves were straightening—his eyes bulging. Why, I wondered, were we eating Hamburger Helper and tuna casseroles? Mama was forever pouring a can of soup over something or another. Trust me. When you see a red-and-white tin of cream o' mushroom soup go on top of chicken—can't nothing good come of the situation.

Part of Mama's amusement with me probably stemmed from the fact that I was dead serious about my arguments. I didn't crack a smile. And I went into some quasi-scientific mix of information to contradict her. Then I think I said something like, "See, the ice melts, proving that it is giving way to the liquid—not the other way around." I am confident that Mama thought I was out of my mind. I used to spend copious amounts of time reading our *Webster's* dictionary and set of *Encyclopedia Britannica* as though they were gripping novels. Often the gems I ran across in those pages informed my liveliest debates. For example, did you know that although most people enjoy eating ice cream on a warm summer day, the summertime favorite actually raises your body temperature? The fat content is the tricky culprit. (I am a blast at cocktail parties with my little fun factoids.)

As you might imagine, the more I flexed my skills of persuasion, the angrier Mama got. And angry Mama was nothing nice. It was clear to me that inside of the next ten minutes or so, she was likely to haul off and backhand me if I didn't pipe down.

She might issue a warning. She might not. It was all in the eyes. Mama had gone off enough that you could easily read the cues. There were times when she was just itching for us to do or say something out of the way. At those moments, she would dare and triple-dare with taunts like "I wish you would" or "If you're feeling froggy—jump," which I never fully comprehended to be completely honest. Roughly translated, it kind of means: "Oh, you bad, huh? Then, c'mon wit' it!" You know that Clint Eastwood movie? The one where he gives the bad guy a flinty-eyed stare and says, "Make my day"? It's that sort of thing.

I don't know this as a qualitative fact, but I don't believe my white friends were getting butt whuppin's like us. In every black home I knew of, a backhand or a belt—or, at least, the threat of a beatdown—informed every parent-child exchange. Fear was a very normal and, presumably, healthy part of family dynamics. Mama was nothing if not thorough. So if there was a dose of fear in the average household, she had to take it up to Mach 5 levels. Mama had a tangible disdain for all things common; ordinary would not cut it.

She was good. Real good. So much so that my brother, my sister, and I lived with a cold, hard truth every day of our existence: Mama was crazy. Not in the Martin Lawrence "you-so-craaazy" kind of way—although Mama proved, at times, that she knew her way around a punch line. No, we were convinced that Old Girl was goo-goo-eyed certifiable. Gone.

In a way, we were right. Now that I have three kids of my own, I am living witness to the cruel truths of insanity.

So I can only imagine Mama, dealing with everything I'm dealing with and then some. Added to her burden was a pretty-boy husband cavorting around town dressed to the nines—or as Dad liked to say, "cleaner than the board of health!" Dad made a good living, working for Dunlop Tire & Rubber faithfully for more than forty years. And he never missed a day of work. Joblessness in a man was something he had no stomach for. It was against his religion. Yet he was so busy being "clean," he often neglected his primary duties as a husband and provider. When Mama grew tired of coming home to find the lights cut off and other foolishness, she left him. Dad came around to visit, but only for fun stuff like taking us to Dairy Queen a few nights a week.

He was Mr. Good Time—all the time. He never disciplined us. Never reprimanded us. And never, ever raised his voice. If we did anything at all to displease him, he might sigh or simply stop talking for a few minutes. He'd actually tried to convince us that we were *supposed* to be happy and have fun, constantly adding, "Your mother has something against a good time. She's a killjoy. Not me." We didn't let on, but even as little kids we knew that was crazy talk.

No matter. He seemed to feel like it was his appointed duty to show his kids the finer things in life. We'd paint the town all the time. In hindsight, I realize that for practical purposes we had to stay on the go. Dad lived with a woman, likely the same one to whom our monthly household funds were diverted. But lest we get the wrong impression, Dad insisted that he was merely a boarder in the woman's house. To add grist to this claim, the woman hummed gospel songs all the time. She was indeed starched and sanctified—evidenced, I suppose, by her horticultural millinery tastes: big elaborate hats with veils, pearls, plastic fowl, fruit, and all manner of silk vegetation atop her self-righteous head. Not that I'm bitter or anything, of course. Occasionally, on our way somewhere, Ms. Holy

Roller would have to ride with us—just long enough for Dad to drop her off at the church for an usher meeting, Bible study, or women's ministry. I have no idea how she rationalized her live-in fellowship with a married man. She'll have to explain that one to her maker.

Perhaps, as a way to compensate for everything his paternal conduct lacked, Dad was preternaturally jolly. So full of jokes and stories he rarely noticed if he was the only one laughing. He wasn't just chipper; homeboy had that Julie-McCoy-*Love-Boat*-cruise-director cheer. With all that skinning and grinning, at six foot five, dressed to the nines 24/7, Dad drew lots of eyeballs—a fact of which he was keenly aware. He enjoyed driving around town for no good reason, sometimes saying, "C'mon, let's see who we can see." Gas was cheap at this point, but when I look back, Dad would sometimes drive around for hours— waving and tooting his horn at folks.

We didn't drive aimlessly all the time. Dad liked to go places. Fancy places. I am sure he inspired the Jay-Z/ Kanye collabo decades later, because if you take away the N-word (he loathed cussing) and other crude references, I can almost hear "Ball so hard" blaring from the eight-track player in Dad's Cadillac. We always went out to eat, often to restaurants where everyone but us had white skin. For casual fare, Dad favored a particular diner in town and we'd stop in just for pie, which I thought was the epitome of high-class living. It was years before I realized that we frequented the place so often because of the nice-looking waitress always on duty. While my face was buried in mountains of canned cherry syrup and pastry flakes—I was always allowed seconds—Dad was getting his Mack on. He took us to professional basketball games, where we saw greats like Dr. J. He even let us hang out in the halls afterward to get autographs. We went to the circus, county fair. You name it.

I cannot even count the number of live concerts we went to. And not just any old concerts; we probably saw Michael Jackson a half dozen times. He didn't squeal along with my sister and I, but I do believe my dad may have loved Michael more than we did. Maybe it was his own headliner frustration or growing up in the racist South. But Dad would pretty much take us to see any top act we admired—as often as we wanted. If it meant driving a few hundred miles, so be it. We never had front-row seats or anything super-duper lavish, but that didn't matter to us. Deep down we knew at the time that, just like the record says: *"We ain't even s'pose to be here . . ."*

We balled so hard, in fact, it was surprising—no, shocking—to learn, as I did from Mama's hushed phone conversations, that Dad seldom delivered child support checks in a timely fashion. She struggled to feed and clothe us. In the midst of our good times, Dad didn't seem to know whether we needed school supplies or had outgrown our sneakers. To keep friction between them to a minimum—or maybe to guilt the old guy—Mama would sometimes have us ask Dad directly to supply the basic needs her paycheck didn't allow. He did, but it was never a pleasant exchange. He'd let out a heavy sigh, like you'd just asked him to spot you a kidney, and ask us how much said item would cost. Even then, I remember thinking: "How is a six-year-old supposed to know the price of a winter coat?"

There were other clues that, perhaps, Dad's charm wore thin. When he came around the house, Papa rarely looked him in the eye. And when he did, it wasn't with the eyes of Christian-like warmth with which he greeted others. Once, when Dad was deep in the throes of an oft-told story about a chance meeting between him and Aretha Franklin, I caught Papa looking at him unkindly. Moments later, Papa retreated to his bedroom and closed the door. Another time, as Dad rhapsodized about his roadie past with gospel greats like the Dixie Hummingbirds, he'd apparently pushed Papa to the edge. My grandfather never spoke ill of anyone. But on this occasion I distinctly heard him mutter to himself, "Anybody talk that much got to be telling lies." I laughed along with Dad, but not quite as vigorously. If something didn't sit right with Papa, it didn't sit right with me.

No wonder Mama operated on a short fuse. She'd had

enough and just wasn't having it with us kids. With a crack of the whip, a pop of the lip, we were a small part of life that she could control.

Well, at least it seemed that way at the time. I suppose compliance reads "control" from the outside. What Mama couldn't possibly see was that she was being played—by each of us in our own way. My brother was a master, for example, of telling Mama whatever she wanted to hear—then doing as he damn well pleased. My sister got some kind of twisted kick out of provoking Mama—pushing the envelope on all presubscribed notions of acceptable behavior. The drama! I can remember praying under my breath: "Dear God, Sissy [that's what we call each other]! Don't test her! It won't end well!"

In one of the few moments I saw Mama cry, it was in response to words spewed by my older sister, as though she wanted to prove in some way that she could go round for round in the verbal slice-and-dice that was Mama's native tongue.

I took a different tack. I'm certainly no mathematician— far from it—but it was a calculated approach that served me well. I'd always been a bit brazen. Mama had smacked me upside the head often. My hide felt the crack of a belt occasionally. And after witnessing beatdown after beatdown when my siblings acted out—which was often—I'd reached a startling conclusion during my preteen years on the planet. Seemed to me that if Mama was going to whup me for *something*, I might as well make it worthwhile.

Every mother has one. In a general household population of well-meaning, law-abiding citizens, there is that kid who is destined to defy, likely to have lip, and generally just prone to piss you off at the drop of a hat. I may have played that role in my house growing up. I didn't really mean to be disrespectful or ill-mannered. I was just unequivocally convinced that I knew more than most every adult on the face of the earth.

I never did anything criminal, mind you. I just decided that fears of a whuppin' were not going to deter me from my appointed teenaged shenanigan duties. If I wanted to skip school, for example, I would simply take a quick mental accounting of how long and intense a beating my infraction might cost me. Usually, the thrill was worth the bill.

I have read all the psychological studies on spanking kids. And I've carefully weighed all the evidence against corporal punishment:

- *It makes children more aggressive later in life.* Totally makes sense that if Mom and Dad beat you, sooner or later you will want to beat somebody too.
- *It curbs kids' cognitive development.* I get this one. If a child doesn't see his parents use reason to solve a problem, why would he?

- *It increases antisocial behavior.* My sibs and I were plenty social, despite our whuppin's, but I guess for some kids all that smacking around might lead you to want more alone time.
- *It inhibits language skills.* I can't be sure where this one comes from. But I am guessing it can't help a kid's vocabulary to constantly hear: "Didn't" *(WHACK)* "I" *(WHACK)* "Tell" *(WHACK)* "You" *(WHACK)* ... over and over again.

I have not undertaken any scientific research of my own. But on a practical level, I can say—without question—that beatings just don't work. If I thought they did some good, even temporarily, I'd be mighty tempted to beat my kids every day. I won't lie or pretend to be holier than thou. Each of my kids will tell you that usually I simply threaten with "You're gonna get it," and they have indeed gotten it a couple of times.

Yes, I probably should've reasoned. In hindsight, I would've achieved more long-lasting results had I talked it out. Helped them understand the error of their ways, and maybe even given them a say in the appropriate consequence.

Oh, well. I'm just not all the way there yet. So if they grow up to be ax murderers—blame me. If they fail to conjugate their verbs properly—blame me. I figure in the end, everything will be my fault anyway. Can't you just see them on a therapist's couch going over my every failing?

- The girls will tearfully reveal that on more than a few occasions, I have looked them dead in the eye and said: "Heifer, I don't have time for your mess today."
- My son will complain that sometimes I scolded, "Boy, don't make me snatch you up . . ."
- Their scars may run deep over the times I yoked them midsentence when they went through their Ebonics phase and I warned through clenched teeth: "You've got one more time to talk like a runaway slave. You hear me?"

The damage has already been done. They would never know it—or appreciate it. But in the discipline department, I am a lightweight compared to Mama. The way their grandmother has mellowed over the past decade or so casts serious doubt over my stories of abuse. To see her now, I almost doubt the past myself. The harsh taskmaster who raised me has morphed into some sort of modern-day fairy-tale character. She goes to church a lot these days. That may have something to do with it. As a teenager, I made Mama promise me she wouldn't turn into one of "those" old ladies. The kind who go to church several times a week and put pink flamingos in the front yard. Nothing against religion, mind you. But why does the Holy Ghost have to arrive now? Couldn't she have called on Jesus forty years ago instead of cussing me out and whupping my behind?

I don't think Mama's beatdowns would work today. Not only because the neighbors would report her to the authorities. Kids are simply too clever these days. And also maybe all the crazy they see on television has desensitized them. I have tried to act as stone-cold cuckoo as possible. And despite it all, my kids don't fear me in the least.

Mama used to say stuff like, "I'll knock you into the middle of next week" and all the other lines for which black parents have become infamous. But while Mama's wild threats seemed to pose a clear and present danger, coming from me the same words fall flat. I can remember when one of my kids—at the age of five or six—so enraged me that I went there. To that place of Mama threats. I squinted my eyes in menacing fashion and I shot back: "I will knock your teeth down your throat!"

She looked at me, quizzically, for a good fifteen seconds and responded: "Mom, that doesn't even make any sense." I had no comeback. She was right. I tried other lines I'd heard Mama say all my life. The one about knocking us into the middle of next week always got our attention as kids. Again, my brood just stared blankly or looked at each other in utter disbelief. A tough crowd, this generation. Nothing scares them. I don't know if it was my delivery or what. Maybe despite my best efforts, I just didn't look crazy enough. Should I bug my eyes? Walk around the house hollering to no one in particular? Come to think of it, Mama did fuss and cuss—long after the actual whaling was over. Without fail, one of them would take a bold, hard look at me and ask, in that exasperated kid way: "What does that even *mean*? Honestly, Mom, where do you get this stuff?"

CHAPTER THIRTEEN

Did I Stutter?

They race down the stairs and round the den, headed toward the laundry room. They need the yellow, not the black, team jersey. The "away" socks are still in the dryer. Players need to arrive early for warmup. The game is in East Jahunga and there's bound to be Parkway traffic.

I'm not studying the people in my house right now. Their Code Blue emergency scramble does not faze me. This is my second cup of coffee—a luxury I mean to savor. It's not easy, especially when the kids look at me with pleading, help-me-look-for-it eyes. I feel for them. But they're on their own. I'm starting to feel my help coming on. Not just in the biblical sense, though that is not to be understated.

I've been asking myself lately—in a David Byrne voice, by the way—"How did I get here?" I'm seriously saying, "This is not my beautiful house." Everything is out of control. Days come and days go and I'm running around like a crazy woman from assignment to assignment. Then I'm dropping one kid off at soccer practice and driving across town to take another to piano lessons. I don't think I'm getting all suburban or anything, but I'm starting to feel like a machine—simply doing a bunch of things, but not really feeling much of anything.

And for what it's worth, I'm beginning to look ratchet, as my girls would say. I never wanted to be one of those women who look good, considering . . . you know, "for having three kids," or "for being middle-aged." I haven't been working out. And I wear sweats, like, every day. It's so bad that the other weekend I went out shopping for shoes and I refused to try on anything that needed lacing or buckling. For the record, I did not come home with Crocs or the clogs that nurses wear (I am not out my natural mind—yet). But I had to catch myself and ask, "Really? You can't tie a pair of shoes? Does your entire life hinge on convenience and mom practicality?" I was ashamed of myself.

A couple of days later, as I was driving to pick up a child—it doesn't matter which one; they're all a blur at this point—I found myself listening to the kids' music, even though I was in the car alone. The song was part rap, part whine—a young dude wailing, "I just wanna be successful." Bruh was like, "*I want the cars and the clothes. The hoes, I suppose.*" It wasn't the misogynist lyrics that caught me—sadly. It was the melody. He was pleading, really. Not the rage-filled spits you normally hear on the radio. I hate to admit it, but the song was quite soothing to my ears at the time.

Then as it played on, there was talking in this sort of monotone voice. The other dude in the collabo came in with verses about, well, I don't know exactly. But it seemed like he was lyricizing about the pitfalls of "that life." Then he said something that struck me. Hard. In fact, I'll never forget it, because whatever he was going on about, this one line was clearly aimed directly at me. For *my* ears. For *my* life. I know now dude's name is Drake and this here is what he said:

"*The game need change. And I'm the [insert expletive] cashier.*" I was like, WHAT????

I was almost ready to testify and do a Holy Ghost dance. It's a good thing I was alone, because I could hardly contain myself at that point. All I could do was yell, "Yasssss! Yasssss!"

I was feeling that line like I have never felt any line before or since. The only thing kinda close would have to be Biggie Smalls, seminal for me in another era, when he said: "Well, if you don't know . . . now you know." But with much respect to the Livest One from Bedford-Stuyvesant, I didn't have kids, a husband, or a grown-up life back then.

So I only thought I was feeling that one. This here Drake line was life itself! *Eeerything!*

Not like a pudgy-faced Canadian could ever unseat B.I.G. or anything like that. But this thing right here? Uh-uh-uh (I'm shaking my head with my eyes closed right now). I'm totally an old head when it comes to hip-hop. But this little boy called Drake can spit quite the catchy rhyme. I can't lie. I sort of like the somewhat wholesomeness he's got going. I guess that means he's soft, but I like it. No gangsta grill. No excessive jewelry. If he has tattoos they aren't all over his body to the point that he looks to have more ink than skin. He is the opposite of Lil Wayne . . . In short, he doesn't look like he stinks.

It's helpful, I find, when you can listen to and watch stuff *with* your kids. Back when I was growing up, Mama and her set listened to much of the same music we kids did. So there was no need for a filter. For example, when the Fatback Band came on, everybody in the house started dancing. Parliament's "Sir Nose D'Voidoffunk" was intergenerational as well. There was lots of innuendo but everybody in the family could listen to the same music. Together. In the same room. Mama didn't need an Urban Dictionary to figure out what we were saying. Not like nowadays. You don't even want to know how long it took me to decipher the whole THOT thing.

But I'm not mad. Due in large part to my young'uns, I'd discovered Drake and got a new lease on life. I started almost right away, making some changes up in here. I began running that type of tight ship I grew up with. Know what I mean?

I worked in the regulation thing gradually, so everybody could have a chance to get with the program. Our family weekends during fall mean only one thing: Soccer. It is a time when Mark comes to life.

Don't get me wrong. He is extremely reliable in his way—eager to take on semioccasional tasks like jerry-rigging toothpick sculptures for a science project or whatever. But he's just not built to last for the classroom-volunteering/carpool-and-playdate-arranging/hormonal-moodswing-checking/thank-you-note-nudging/doctor-appointment-making/permission-slip-signing/field-trip-chaperoning/Instagram-monitoring/teacher-gift-contrib-uting/lunchbox-packing grind of everyday parenthood.

The fleeting weeks of soccer season, however, are different. Games, Gatorade, and gear bring out a whole new Dad. He acquires new and enhanced skill sets. In the hours leading up to kickoff, for example, Mark displays an uncanny ability to foreshadow events. Often on weekdays if I need to rush home from work, pick one child up from aftercare, drop another off at practice, and attend a back-to-school night meeting that starts at six P.M., he won't necessarily wrap his head around the idea of dinner and homework.

On weekends, though, his head is totally in the game. The only thing missing is a chalk diagram. Like a seasoned playmaker I notice him anticipating most every eventuality. He packs an inordinate amount of just-in-case items. And not just the obvious like an extra jacket. He carries plastic bags in the event juices spring a leak or clothes get messy. He ventures into ShopRite, days in advance, to buy snacks. Healthy ones, like whole-grain bars, fruit, and cheese. Then—and here is where I'm blown away—these things are placed in a cooler, with ice packs. Let's just say the sporting pursuits of his kids are very important. Something (he is fond of reminding me) I know nothing about.

What's funny—not in a "ha-ha" way—is that as critical as their organized play is, getting out the door is anything but. Most always, some major element goes missing. I am a disinterested spectator during these scrambles. My motto is "A place for everything and everything in its place." I find visits to joints like the Container Store to be near-orgasmic experiences. I've bought the kids cheap drawer dividers to separate their jerseys, shorts, and socks from everyday clothes—making all the game accouterments neat and accessible. And I placed a HomeGoods wicker bin by the back door exclusively for cleats and shin guards to be deposited after games. Does anyone bother to follow The System? Of course not. So in their frenzied hunts, I figure the best response is no response at all. Thus, it is during these moments they turn to Dad, who is the official mascot, quarterback, and captain of their search-and-rescue team.

"Yes!" Apparently the all-important yellow jersey has been identified and located. Chloe and her dad are all set to leave . . . Or so they think.

I am forced to break my silence at this point: "Chloe, you do know you're not going anywhere without cleaning the bathroom. Right?"

Initially, she flashes a smirk so filled with preteen swagger you can almost hear her defiant eyes say: "*So long, sucka!*" Her dad doesn't move. He stands frozen with indignation. Words fail him. He lets out a heavy sigh and looks skyward as if to say, *Help me, Lord. Help me.*

Sensing that Daddy can't "save" her, equal parts shock and suddenly brim confusion in baby's brown eyes. Father and daughter both exchange glances and their faces synchronize in a "Can you BELIEVE this woman?!" look of annoyance.

In desperation, Chloe whines, "*Mom, I gotta gooooo-ah!*"

"Sorry, boo. The bathroom's your job this week and I told you to get on it three hours ago." Naturally, I got all the 'tude you can imagine—exasperated sighs, teeth sucking, eye rolling. And Chloe wasn't too happy with me either. Girlfriend brings the drama as only she can with her toilet-seat slamming and furious Windex-brandishing self. But an adolescent hormonal spectacle is nothing I can't handle.

Cleaning the bathroom is not something I just sprung on Chloe. Honestly, I leave no room for confusion when it comes to these matters. It wasn't always like this.

I used to scream—a *lot*. Not that I was particularly angry. Well, sometimes I was. It's just that everyone in my house seems to have selective hearing. Our home is a decent size—there's the main floor, upstairs, a basement—but by no means grand. When I speak, I know that they know that I know they hear me. But hours later I get some version of this: "Huh? What? I didn't know I was supposed to . . . You never told me . . . What happened?"

Sometimes, I'm sure the act of bewilderment was a cruel hoax. But I really believe that often the ignorance was real. It would drive me crazy. So crazy I began to wonder whether I'd ever said what I said I said—thought I said, knew I said. Seriously, it felt as though the whole household was hell-bent on killing me softly. So I switched things up a bit. I began to get in their faces. I was like *Rush Hour*'s Chris Tucker in that crazy scene where he goes, "*DO YOU UNDERSTAND THE WORDS THAT ARE COMING OUT OF MY MOUTH?*" That didn't work out too well either.

Then I wised up . . . Got all Supernanny up in here—making charts and lists, sticky notes, texting reminders. I didn't announce the big shift. In my own mind, I just decided that like Kurtis Blow always said, it was time to "*Break it up; Break it up; Break it up—Break DOWN!*"

It is laughable to me that my kids think their little jobs are so burdensome. Mama is oh-so-mellow these days that they think I'm lying when I tell them what I and their aunt and uncle were responsible for. They gripe about unloading the dishwasher when we were busting suds every single day—sometimes, twice a day.

Inside the pantry door I taped two printouts, clearly delineating everyone's chores. My two daughters swap weekly from Floor to Dishes duty. Every element of each job is spelled out. Cole can't read so well yet. So instead of a list, he gets a picture of a garbage can. And he knows that means he is to empty the wastebaskets throughout the house. I think when he is about seven or so, I'll have him take the cans to the curb on garbage day.

DAILY CHORES

DISHES*	FLOOR**
Unload clean items from dishwasher	Clear and clean kitchen table
Rinse and load dirty ones, placing all like items (especially silverware) together	Organize shoes on shoe mat, removing excess pairs (no one should have more than two pairs downstairs)
Clean countertops surrounding sink	Swiffer kitchen floor thoroughly
Clean sink and mat with sponge and disinfectant cleanser	Clean island with sponge and disinfectant cleanser
Clean drain and drain catch with same	Take out garbage

*On Saturday, person on DISHES duty cleans downstairs bathroom (Lysol mandatory) and vacuums downstairs, including den, hallway, and staircase

**On Saturday, person on FLOOR duty cleans pink bathroom upstairs, puts throw rugs in washer/dryer; disinfects floor

NOTE: In addition to assigned tasks, you must make your bed daily and clean your room on a weekly basis—putting all clothes, shoes, books, etc. in their appropriate places.

I know this all seems extremely anal-retentive. But there is no shame in my game. I'll tell anybody, lists like these are the bomb.com. So clear. So simple. As a writer I may be biased, but I swear there is just nothing like the printed word. No matter how a person tries to twist it, turn it, or otherwise manipulate it for their own devices—words stand true. They seem to stare you down and say, *"What? No, you didn't just try to play me!"*

When she emerges about ten minutes later, I make a point of telling Chloe she did a good job on the bathroom when, in truth, the cleaning was fair at best. I know I can be tough, but I'm not trying to be a total shrew.

I'll be the first to admit that all this chore-chart-consistent-consequences stuff is an all-day-every-day job. I am not trying to say it requires advanced intellect or superhuman powers. But it is not easy. There is only one reason I am even halfway equipped to take on the role: I am my mama's child.

My siblings and I grew up under a high set of expectations—probably too high and with fierce reprisals. We were allowed to play and do some normal kid things but not until the kitchen floor was clean and the bathroom faucets gleamed. We thought everyone had to clean the garage—not just tidy it up, scrub it down. We were the only kids on the block I ever saw regularly hosing and sweeping the sidewalk.

More than just chores, Mama was giving us—in her mind—moral fiber. Just as important as a job well done was character, namely self-control and honesty. She was real big on the truth. Lord, Lord, Lord, please don't let

Mama catch you in a lie. She would not only threaten to "whoop your black ass," you had to endure her scorn—and the latter strike inflicted far more pain: "Nothing in this world is worse than a low-down dirty liar—nothing!"

Was Mama too hard on us? Did she beat us too much? Cuss too much? Given where she came from and what she experienced, I don't think so. Her generation knew that kids, especially black kids, needed solid home training to survive in the world. They knew that the oppression from The Man, Mister Charlie—all things Establishment—would not likely judge us fairly. Under such merciless scrutiny we had to be smarter. Our behavior had to be better. Our clothes and bodies had to be cleaner. And above all, we had to be stronger than any children on the face of the earth. We had to be prepared to withstand the wrath of racism that would surely meet us in adulthood.

Okay, I realize this is not 1978. I know the nation has elected a black man as leader of the free world. Twice. And I am well aware that our First Lady cuts a cocoa-brown, elegant, graceful, and intelligent figure whose polished countenance screams class. And at the same time it whispers, "But don't try me."

Like black women the world over, I'm proud Mrs. O went to Princeton. I'm pleased that she has had a high-powered career. However, just as satisfying—and black

women won't say this in mixed company, but I'll spill it—
is that Mrs. Obama has Sister Style. She rocks Jason Wu
and keeps a tight 'do (no offense, Condoleezza). No ma-
tronly roller set. No messy weaves. No jacked-up kitchen
(you'll just have to ask somebody about that; I'm not telling everything here). We couldn't love her more if she
were our own blood kin.

My own personal appreciation for her goes even deeper
though. Our sister-girl friendship grew steadily throughout the 2008 campaign. The deal was sealed after the in-
auguration, when she moved her mother into the White
House and made it clear that her girls would be getting a
small allowance, making their beds, and watching little or
no TV.

This confirms it. The First Lady of the United States is
my homegirl! Clearly, 'Chelle (I know she would let me
call her that in private) is a for-real-mama kind of mom.
I'm not suggesting that Sasha and Malia scrub the White
House's thirty-five bathrooms. But the point is, FLOTUS
is not playing. Even secure in the knowledge that her kids
can easily get good government jobs—with benefits, she
pushes them. I respect that.

I don't know if her husband is constantly blocking like
most. But I do know she has a lot on her plate. Staying on
top of kids is very time-consuming, draining, and thank-

less. I'm the Enforcer. That is my assigned role in the house. I have grown to accept that as far as my family is concerned, I get off on making their dad and Chloe or Trinity late for the game. Perhaps I'm enjoying a cheap contact high from the strong smell of Scrubbing Bubbles wafting from the bathroom.

The truth is, I have a lot of friends who—I suspect—find my thing with regulation a little weird. Some of my girlfriends say things like, "I don't have the energy. Good for you." I'm not looking for a gold star or a biscuit. And I'm not throwing rules around for sport. As my kids get older, I've had very frank discussions with them about race and society's expectations. I am happy to live in a multi-race community. And I am eternally grateful to see that my kids' friendship circles represent a variety of ethnicities. But I'm not ready to break out in Kumbaya harmony just yet. It is a white world. And as Papa Pope reminded Olivia and the rest of America in *Scandal*'s third season: *"You've got to be twice as good to get half of what they have."* Old-school black-parent-speak, for sure, but it's not all that far off from the truth.

I don't think my kids have ever been subject to outright racism. I don't think a teacher has ever suggested they set their sights lower than their white peers. Quite the contrary. My kids have had awesome teachers—teachers who have taken the time to nudge, push, and shove them to do their best.

It doesn't always work. Still, I say woe unto the black parents in liberal and "diverse" towns like mine who fail to prepare their black children for the realities of a racist society. Really, though, while our skin shade adds another layer to the rule-setting thing, all kids need discipline. My kids actually *like* the structure I provide. You'll never hear them say, "More rules, Mommy! Please, more rules!" But while lots of moms and dads are being their kid's friend, I get to see how proud the kids are when I come home to a clean kitchen (not often, but still) and laud them with praise. They miss out on the joy and pride at those times when they get a C on a midterm—yet weeks later, manage (with some prodding from me) to press in and ace their final.

The stern side of me is balanced out with plenty of love and affection. I shower kisses on all three of my kids until they order me to stop. I don't hope they know I love them. I tell them constantly that not only do I adore them but they are the very best part of me.

It's not a parenting tactic or a self-esteem-building trick. My kids are just mad cool peeps, better company than most adults. When I'm not laying down the law—which is only on an as-needed basis—my kids and I dance to old-school hip-hop. I've decided that God gave Trinity a double dose of rhythm to make up for Mama's lack. She can hang with the baddest of video dancers. Cole's pop-and-lock is coming along nicely. And, of course, Chloe is "Terror Squad" cool—*lean back, lean back, lean back.* On Fridays we watch movies. Sometimes we play cards or board games.

I'm a very regular mom. I just don't take no mess.

CHAPTER FOURTEEN

They Call It Stormy Monday (. . . but Tuesday's Just as Bad)

The blues doesn't come around me all that often. But when it does darken my door, it's never a polite visitor.

It is ornery. And it is brazen—reminding me of a sloppy drunk. Growing up, Mama used to have card parties with her girlfriends. They all smoked back then. The blues busts in my house like one of those Kool Mild–puffing women—on a night when the effects of Jim Beam conspire with the constraints of polyester leisure suits and the vagaries of pinochle. I know I seem like a tough chick. I talk a lot of smack. But the truth is I'm no match for this kind of heartache. Nothing—neither my research, my reporting, nor my mama's rhetoric—prepared me. See, my blues is just so many things. Mostly, it's confusing. I am now the mother of not one, not two, but three—count 'em—healthy and beautiful children. Cole only got here a short time ago, but it's clear that God put him here to be the cherry on my already delicious ice cream sundae. The girls love having him around and they are eager to help out in any way they can. Yet, inexplicably less than two years in, your sister-girl is weary, y'all. I'm through.

Like most everyone's blues, mine has a certain sorrow. But it is also belligerent with a capital *B* and it waves its messy patheticness all up in my face—scowling, cussing, crying, breath stinking, cigarette dangling. Let me tell you, this here blues can show out! I'm trying to tell you. For no particular reason that leaps to mind, I think I might just cut somebody today.

Now I wonder: Does the blues act up like this, so bold and nasty, when it comes calling at a white woman's house? I don't think so. (If you are a white woman who does, in fact, get the dirty, low-down blues, I apologize in advance, my sister.)

This morning, at around 6:20 A.M., a blunt-force misery woke up with me. Then it had the nerve to sit its mean self down at the kitchen table and share my coffee. I can't shake the nagging suspicion that, while uninvited, it's fixing to hang around for a good while. And there is not a damn thing I can do about it.

Lord knows I'm trying. For the sake of the kids, I want to pull it together. It would be nice if the people I am charged to love and nurture didn't have to start their day with Miss Evilene LeFunk. They don't deserve this. I know one of them will set me off this morning. One of them will start in with something asinine like, "We don't have any orange juice, Mommy?" And I'll have to just snap. Both good humor and good sense will momentarily take leave and I'll scream, *"Do you SEE any orange juice? Do I look like a Florida citrus tree to you? Do I? Well, it looks like you're in for a day without sunshine, boo. Okay? Deal with it!"*

Of course, their eyes will get all big and spooked and they will be emotionally scarred—for life, or at least until I apologize fifteen minutes later. Dang. I really hate it when this blues comes on me. It is in these moments that the cat is let out of the proverbial bag. And my children know, *really* know, their otherwise loving and devoted mother is all kinds of cray-cray.

I should probably lie down. That would help. I need, um . . . honestly, I don't know what I need. But sleep does work wonders. Last night I didn't get any—sleep (or the other stuff on your dirty mind)—and sadly, that is not all that unusual. I am really, really, really tired. I am a whole lot of other things. But let's start there. I'm tired.

No one seems to want to let me be tired, to admit that I am human. I know I'm not by myself. Kids get to take naps. Dads get to tune out and feign ignorance. But mothers suffer the Energizer Battery Syndrome. A woman I work with, Erika, told me the other day that her husband was complaining about the hard day he'd put in at work. She told him, "You went to an office and stayed there all day and practically all night. I went to an office, came home, did laundry, cooked, cleaned up—because the kids' breakfast bowls and spoons that were on the table when I left this morning were still there when I came back, even though you leave after me—and made lunches for tomorrow. I took the kids to the dentist too. You're having a rough day? Shut up! I'm Puerto Rican. I didn't have a rough day; I have a rough life!"

That woman is now my hero. When she told me, although I'd known her for just three weeks at the time, I decided we'd be friends for life.

I know men do get tired. I get that they, too, work hard. But I don't think they can comprehend a woman's utter bone fatigue. Woman to woman, we have to feel each other's pain. We should be there for one another. I always thought Oprah was that for me—you know, in my corner. It was traumatic, I can remember, the first time I came to realize that Oprah Winfrey was very, very different from me. I know what you're thinking, "The talk show, magazine, and gazillion-dollar bank account didn't tip you off?" Putting aside her uber success, I always thought she was feeling a regular sister like myself. I really did.

Then, years ago, I listened as one of those fluffy entertainment show reporters interviewed Oprah about con-

tinuing her show. This was pre-OWN and Sweetie Pie
and Iyanla. They asked the TV mogul if she was tired of
doing her talk show. And her response bugged me. She
waxed on, with rich gravitas—switching from her girlfriend voice to the anchorwoman timbre she uses when
she's about to get deep (all black folks are bilingual in a
way, so I'm not mad at her for that). She started in about
slavery and the history of our people. She always brings up
Sojourner Truth at times like this. Her point was that because of the suffering of our foremothers, who had no
voice, she had no right to be tired. She reasoned that just
as they kept picking cotton and going on, so should a
woman like her. She can't quit, because they had no voice,
no rights . . . you get the idea.

It was beautiful in a way. I certainly appreciate Oprah's
consciousness and her truth. The woman speaks the truth.
She has achieved phenomenal success, of course, but she
never forgets The Struggle. She is philanthropic and outspoken in a way that most black celebrities of her status are
not. I never heard Michael Jordan comment on how poor
inner-city kids were warring over his pricey sneakers. Did
you? He seemed to say, "Wear my kicks by any means necessary." So that doesn't count as black consciousness. Do
you see Beyonce giving out weaves to the less fortunate
among us? Forget about Jay-Z. Probably it *was* a hard-
knock life once upon a time. But now dude steady reminds

us he's "got extensive hoes . . . expensive clothes." I swear if that mofo tells us one more time about his Maybach—so help me!

I really count on Oprah. Call me corny. But she is my hero . . . really holds it down for a sister.

And, I'm sorry if this is wrong of me. Too much pressure to put on one woman's shoulders, perhaps. But I really needed her to represent in that moment. With a nod to our black history and all the courageous souls who came before us, maybe in her *Color Purple* dialect, she could've spoken up for the hardworking sisters in the present. Maybe she could've muttered, Sofia-like: "Yaaassa. I's be *tiiide* some time. Stedman and Gayle work my last nerve. And you know, I got all dem dogs and all dem houses and all dis money to keep up wit' till I just be wo' *out*!" That would've done a lot for me. Seriously, she could've saved me and countless others during that interview. I still want her to say it. Be honest. It's okay if she doesn't yell it to the rooftops like she does when she gives away cars and cashmere house slippers. She can whisper it . . . *Shhh!* We will keep it on the low, girlfriend; the ancestors will never have to know.

Then again, maybe the O really doesn't get tired. Maybe when she and Gayle are road-tripping across country grubbing on cheese fries and singing off-key, they don't know about those of us who spend our days cooking and pretreating shit-streaked underwear before trudging to office cubicles and then doing the same thing in reverse the next day. I do recall hearing somewhere that after Oprah and Gayle clocked four hundred miles or so driving out West, they stayed at a fancy hotel in Las Vegas—without VIP treatment. Apparently, Oprah emerged from the ten- or fifteen-minute check-in process and said, "Whew, this normal way of doing things is time-consuming, huh?"

Trust me, I am not hating on the wealthiest and most powerful woman in the world. I love me some Oprah Winfrey and I always have. I even wrote her a fan letter back in the day when she was broadcast only in Chicago— and I still have her purple, hand-signed response. So I've got love for this woman. Okay? I'm just desperate, that's all, for someone to hear my pain.

It's not going to happen. I know that now. Ever since we left Brooklyn I had come to a new appreciation of the crazy, desperate antics of seemingly normal housewives who end up on the evening news. Not that I ever considered running a meth lab or having a scandalous affair with my kids' twenty-something soccer coach (FYI, the boy is *foine* and has a British accent). It's just that motherhood isolation? It's a real thing.

On the bright side, I should probably be glad the blues showed up at all. Otherwise I'd be completely alone. Even when the kids and an army of friends are running all through the house and even when Mark comes home, this is a lonely life at times. Kids don't do grateful . . . it's not in their job description. When they signed up for this gig, it was with the full and open understanding of their primary function: Drain your mama to within an inch of her very life. Being the great kids they are, mine do their level best to live up to their duties.

In fairness, it's not their fault. For some reason, a lot of the time I feel as though I'm swimming upstream. And if you don't know it already, Olivia Pope (note sister-girl's Esther Williams swim cap) notwithstanding, black women are generally not trying to get with swimming on a regular basis (having to do with the fact that whether we are weaved, relaxed, or natural, salt and chlorine do a number on our hair. Plus, we can't be bothered. We've got enough troubles.)

This is a lot. Have I mentioned that I'm old? Let's acknowledge that piece. Maybe not Methuselah, old-as-dirt old or decrepit. But, despite my girlish charms, I've got some years on me. I do not think women over forty are really designed for babies. Yet I do indeed have a baby—a toddler who, like most, wants his mama. ALL. THE. TIME. I also have two tween girls—who have attitude for days and never want, but sorely need, their mama. ALL. THE. TIME. If I am to keep them from aspiring to be like some sorry, silicone-injected reality-show tarts and keep them off the pole, I must keep these two chicks in check. ALL. THE. TIME.

A week or so ago, in a desperate state of frustration, I tried to express to Mark just what I was going through, because despite the fact that I'm probably OVERsharing in these pages, I don't routinely do a whole lot of opening up. That can likely be traced back to the words I heard Mama say often growing up—"People got their own shit to deal with. Don't go around giving them any of yours." So full of wisdom, that Mama. Still, I thought as husband and wife we should strive toward greater communication and better understanding (although I'm not sure he was of the same mind). Anyway, I thought at the very least, I should try to give some context for my wretched disposition. So I sat him down: The situation is dark—very dark, I explained. With methodic detail I laid out my fatigued-lonely-overwhelmed-and-underappreciated feelings. Men function best with specifics, so I basically went through all the reasons why I felt I was morphing into Grandmaster Flash (*"Don't push me cuz I'm close to the edge; I'm tryin' not to lose my head. A-huh-huh-huh."*).

I didn't actually spit the verses, but I did tell him that half the time I couldn't tell if I'm going crazy or coming back. I poured out my heart for a good fifteen minutes, again with details (because men always say "be specific, not emotional")—there's Cole's thumb-sucking I need to address, the girls' pending puberty, and so on. He heard little after the word *crazy*. That was somewhat entertaining, I suppose, and so he said something like, "I've been telling you all this time that you're a little crazy. That's funny." He enjoyed a good laugh—thus concluding our heart-to-heart.

I had to pray myself down from going Joe Pesci on his behind—thus leaving my children daddyless, black statistics. You know that scene in *Goodfellas*, when he says: "You think I'm funny? Do I amuse you in some way? Funny how?" I can't recall, but I am pretty sure in wiseguy fashion the unsuspecting chuckler gets blown away. Not that I could ever be so violent. I'm just saying.

What would any normal person find funny about my heartache? Now that I think about it, my husband's comedic instincts (if we can call them that) have been rubbing me the wrong way for a while now. Wife jokes are big with Mark. You will never see him laugh harder than when Chris Rock stand-up specials air on TV. I don't know Mr. Rock, of course, nor do I know much about his personal life. But it seems to me that much of his gags have to do with women—how conniving we are, how annoying we are, and, in so many words, how useless we are. Often the send-ups circle back to his wife. (I believe TMZ recently reported that the comedian and wifey are splitsville. Coincidence? I think not.) They are "just jokes," Mark likes to remind me.

I'm no expert, but I think it's safe to say that in matters of funny—or even matters of unfunny—timing is everything. Last night, as bedtime approached, I was doing what I usually do—wrangling the kids to finish their homework, shower, and get to bed. The blues had not yet made its formal entrance, but I think it was clear from the way I was screaming and snapping that storm clouds were brewing.

I went to bed with a slowly festering funk. Then the for-real thing began sometime in the middle of the night—okay, 2:47 A.M., to be exact. That's around the time when Cole's big-boy-bed ambivalence usually kicks in. He toddled into our room (the same way he did two nights ago) and his little fingers tapped my shoulder—always the adorable digits tap *me*. His dad's side of the bed is clearly the shorter, most direct route from the doorway, but he makes a beeline for Mommy. In these predawn moments I'm too bleary-eyed sleepy to play enforcer and even at two and a half he knows it. So he hoists himself into the bed. I'd like to say he snuggles next to me, but that would not be an accurate report of what happens next. Like Gorilla Glue adhesive, the pint-sized interloper affixes his small frame to mine—with a bony knee or elbow ensconced in my lower back—then settles in for the night.

The good news is, Cole nods off pretty quickly after his stealth entry. Sometimes I do too. He doesn't toss, turn, or perform any sort of nocturnal contortionist routine. Trinity, at his age, used to lie in a perpendicular state of repose so rigid I could barely lift her twenty-pound body. The not-so-good news for me is that over the course of the night Cole somehow manages to scoot his body toward me to the point where we are not just close to one another; we are fused, conjoined even. I can't turn over or even move my arms. His slow but steady entrenchment means that by four A.M. or so I am struggling to protect a personal sleep zone of about twelve square inches.

Meanwhile, on the other side of the bed lies Mark. He is resting comfortably, arms boldly splayed to either side and snoring like a wanton caveman. It's not his fault, I guess, that he didn't sense Cole rousing out of his bed hours earlier. That he didn't hear the late-night creep. That he didn't feel the third-party presence of this adorable and wily little creature right under his nose.

And who can blame Cole? The baby can't help being blessed with the inborn skill to intrude strategically— carefully choosing his dead-of-night target. His mama ain't raising no fool. When he left the hospital and crossed the threshold some thirty months ago, he likely got the memo from his sisters: "Whilst there are two adults occupying this house, one is not to be disturbed, interrupted,

or otherwise inconvenienced by your fleeting wishes, requirements, or wants—especially if said wishes, wants, and
requirements occur after normal business hours."

Once thoroughly and irreversibly wide awake, I take
note on the way to the bathroom that my house is tore up,
from the floor up. I mean it is a holy mess. I don't mean
just a bit untidy. No one up in this joint thinks anything
has to be put away.

Lego holes are permanently embedded into the soles of
my feet. Books lie everywhere *but* the bookshelves. The
kitchen floor looks like somebody's been crying on it, as
Mama used to say. (I never quite got that expression, but
the gist is clear.) For a black woman from back in the day,
cleanliness is truly next to godliness. That's not just some
tired saw. It's a sister's truth. Now might be a good time to
tell the world that black people, especially us women, are
convinced that we are the cleanest people on the face of
the earth. If you ever invite a black woman to your house
for dinner and she says she's not hungry or appears to
be simply moving the food around on her plate, it is because she holds a sneaking suspicion that you took the
raw chicken out of the store packaging without so much as
a rinse. She is also secretly questioning whether you even
washed your hands before you began cooking. Within
minutes of entering your home she has probably scoped
your tile grout and your dish drain—the well-raised

among us know that bad boy has to be emptied and disinfected on the regular.

Mama would size up a woman's cleaning game. Quick fast. And her judgment was irrevocable. You couldn't feign ignorance. You were to have no off days. I can still remember Mama on our Princess phone gossiping to her friends. A woman in the neighborhood could be screwing half the eastern seaboard, but if her spot was clean, she got some bonus points. Mama might say, "She is a grade-A whore-ish tramp. She keeps a nice house, though. Have you seen her windows?" On the other hand, no amount of church-going or class could right a woman who didn't get down with Mr. Clean. You weren't just a bit scattered or untidy. You were "nasty" (extra-strong emphasis on the first syllable) and a "dirty shame" if you couldn't get your domestic duties tight.

Mama spent many a Saturday morning catching up with her friends, and I can hear her now, with Sugar on the other end of the line:

> "Uh-huh . . . It looked kind of clean. But did you see all that dirt caked up in the corners of the floor? Hmmph . . . She hasn't touched those base-boards in months . . . And the walls were just as dingy as could be. She probably wiped the windows a few times, but she sure as hell didn't use

vinegar. Those windows look like somebody's been crying on them.

"It's a shame too, because she's very attractive. She could use a good girdle, though—and I mean a good one. She was wearing that jumpsuit. With a good girdle it wouldn't have looked so cheap. Too bad her husband's whore-hopping around. She's probably so busy trying to keep that fool . . . She needs to be cleaning that nasty house, if you ask me."

I know I can't speak for all black women, but I can say that I have never met a sister (and I don't think I ever will) who would hang one of those quaint placards on her walls with Erma Bombeck–like quotes—*God bless this mess.* Our black mamas have taught us that the good Lord don't like dirt. If he did, he wouldn't have invented Pine-Sol. Most of the time I can walk—even strut—in my feminist talk. But days like today, the funk in my head mixed in with the dust and clutter up in my house makes me feel like a total loser. What kind of woman lives like this? Why can't I get my *-ish* together?

Of course, it doesn't take Sigmund Freud to figure out that the house is just pretext. That's what I mean about this blues. It turns me into a sour, rambling fool. I mean I *love* my family. Praise God and Hallelujer! I am blessed—

"too blessed to be stressed," and all the rest (*that's* the placard sisters hang, because God forbid we admit to being burdened).

Deep, deep down I know they are all **guileless** innocents—these folks in my charge. It's not as though they hatched some grand scheme to make me suffer. It's not their problem that while they all lie nestled in a deep, pleasant slumber I am left clinging, desperate and white-knuckled, to the edge of a king-sized bed.

But just because I can't find evidence of conspiratorial plotting doesn't mean I'm not mad.

I'm mad. And I am very, very tired. I'm so tired that I'm sick.

And, you know what? I'm sick and tired of being sick and tired!

CHAPTER FIFTEEN

A Brand-New Bag

Mama never put a whole lot of expectations on my siblings and me. I know it may seem on the surface like some brand of reverse psychology. But I doubt that. Mama didn't put things in reverse, or sideways, or even parallel. Even as an adult, when I try to—delicately and respectfully—suggest that she couch things a bit more softly, she usually responds, "Ain't nobody got time for all that."

For example: In recent years, Mama's charm and good looks have drawn the attention of a couple of potential suitors. Not that she has ever wanted for attention. Mama is not playing, and never has been, when it comes to the way she altogether puts it together. Firstly, the good Lord made her fine. And I'm not just saying that because she's my mama. Her clothes, while not always expensive, fit her just right. Don't think that just because she got up every day to go to a factory job, she got up and dressed like she was getting ready to go to a factory job. Nowadays, we'd call her look "business casual." Mama usually wore polyester slacks or bell-bottom jeans—pressed, of course—and any one of an array of colorful blouses. Mama was sorta kinda lacking in the hip department. Okay, truth be told, her figure went straight up and down, with big boobs attached. But she worked it like a Shanté supermodel. She was very, very, very conscious of her weight. I clearly recall strange food combinations being touted as weight-loss formulas, like the grapefruit-spinach–boiled egg diet. Also, I have vivid memories of her wearing what looked like giant garbage bags around the house to "melt" her weight off. Her poundage hardly seems an issue. In fact, Mama has worn a size ten my entire life.

She had her share of beaus. My favorite, hands down, was the short, pudgy guy who owned a candy store. His store sold more than candy, but that was all that mattered to me. E was a good guy in many ways and he loved Mama a lot. My point is, she was never pressed for dating options. Any old way, a few years ago there was a seemingly lovely gentleman from church who was smitten. Let's call him Tom. It's random. It sounds white. And, coincidentally, he happens to be white. Not the first time in the snow for Mama, who has always taught us to never judge anyone by the color of their skin. If I might digress, that may explain why I've never had a problem with the black-white dating thing that gets so many sisters upset. I'm not angry with a brother who doesn't want me. I feel bad for you, son; but I'm not angry. If someone always dates outside their race, that's something different. Some self-hateration going on, if you know what I mean.

Okay, so Mama and Tom had a date. He was planning to take her to a cookout with his friends and family on a lovely Saturday afternoon. Unfortunately, Mama later explained to me, when Tom arrived at the door, she had to "tell him 'bout himself"—her way of saying she read old boy like a dog-eared tabloid. I couldn't understand how the date ended before it even began. You, too, may wonder: What egregious act could poor Tom have committed before he even crossed Mama's threshold?

Apparently, the old white dude had the gall to roll up looking like an old white dude. And not a dressed-up old white dude, wearing the after-five uniform of Dockers and a polo. Tom had on jeans that, I'm guessing, weren't pressed. A shirt with something written on it. Mama didn't go for graphic T-shirts for people half Tom's age. For reasons known to sweet Jesus alone, she felt compelled to tell Tom he looked a hot mess. And, for heaven's sake, he couldn't go anywhere with her dressed like that. Even in the retelling, Mama was genuinely surprised that Tom took offense. Sadly, their romance went downhill after that.

I say all this to say that Mama's language was seldom nuanced. She meant what she said, and she said what she meant. When she insisted that all she wanted was for us to be happy and "do good," we had little reason to doubt her. Careerwise, she added just one caveat: "I don't care if you turn out to be a ditchdigger—be the best ditchdigger you know how."

Here lately, as I sat around my computer in ratty sweat-pants, a part of me wondered whether I was in fact living up to her simple wish. Was this really my best? Working from home meant working more, not less. Being off-site as an independent contractor meant being "on" at all times, as if every day were your first day on the job—which is sort of like being married and acting like you are on a protracted first date. "Do they like me—really like me?" I'd find myself asking. "Where is our relationship headed?" "Will I write just this one piece?" "Will they consider me for a regular contributorship?"

You can never get comfortable. You operate in a weird space of uncertainty about everything, not just job security—although that is the biggest consideration. What was the editor not telling you about an assignment? Were you the first choice, or had several others already turned it down? Did she really know what she wanted from the article, or was she sending you on a fishing expedition for whatever came up?

I was certainly laboring like a ditchdigger. Emotionally if not physically. Working from home means gaping holes of fraught silence. Ever stared at your inbox or refreshed again and again wishing for a ping? I don't recommend it. No one picks up a phone anymore. So if it just so happened that a storm hit or Verizon had declared another intermittent service outage, my neighbors were slightly inconvenienced. I, on the other hand, would be left teetering on the verge of a nervous breakdown. Even with FiOS speed, my problems were not eliminated. As a sole means for "conversation," e-mail can be complicated, because it leaves room for lots of ambiguity. It's easy to come off as confrontational and abrupt online. There are no smiles, no inflections, no laughter.

I could get an e-mail from an editor and stew for hours—trying to figure out a response. More often than not, there was no appropriate response that would keep my job safe.

I got a missive from an editor once that got me really fired up, mostly because it was a commentary on my professionalism—or, in her opinion, lack thereof. We'd actually worked together for some time. She'd hired me to work at a parenting website she oversaw. To this day, I'm not sure how, as a childless person, she pulled off a gig as editorial director for so long. But it did explain why so much of the content seemed so vacuous. When I got there, the site had lost its leadership status; unique visits were down and newer sites were grabbing all the views as well as the industry buzz. She was professional enough and very capable in her way. But she was talking to mothers all wrong. It's not only that she lacked kids, I think she lacked perspective—living in the city, surrounded by families who had absolutely nothing in common with folks in the rest of the country.

I was managing a holiday package as a freelancer for the site—developing blog and story ideas, assigning pieces, editing them. It wasn't going well. Apparently, the advertiser came through sometime in October and wanted the entire vertical up and running in around three weeks' time. My boss expected the market person I'd contracted to come up with a gift guide for kids filled with "unique" toys and accessories. I thought the woman I assigned was great. She'd worked at *Cookie*, a cool parenting magazine that never managed to find enough hipster parents to buy it, and had a great eye. My editor found something wrong with most everything she submitted. At one point, she even insisted on featuring her own absurd choices—like a cardboard dollhouse that sold for nearly two hundred dollars. (I later read the comments section; trust me, moms in Peoria were not impressed.)

I didn't like some of my boss's product choices, but I was a big girl about the gift guide part. To me, gadget advice and features like "Looks We Love" aren't even journalism. Just filler. So, whatever. The articles, though, were like my babies. And girlfriend had the gall to send back a story I'd edited "sloppily," in her view. She highlighted a sentence that read something like: "Moms have myriad choices this holiday season." In Track Changes mode, she typed, "Where's the 'of'? Basic stuff here . . ."

Sadly what the editrix didn't know was that *myriad* is both a noun and an adjective. *Of* is actually not required in proper usage. I thought, *How dare she?* But there is no nice way to debate something like that by e-mail without coming off as uppity.

Have you ever heard that great Winston Churchill quote? I think it was Winston Churchill. It was an old white guy respected by many, who once said: "Tact is the ability to tell someone to go to hell in such a way that they enjoy the trip." That was what I needed. I can sometimes summon the wherewithal to pull it off. But I had just twenty minutes before the girls would come home from school and Cole was in the next room crying. My life sucked. Big-time.

My accidental career and I had reached an impasse. This touchy juncture reminded me of middle school romances. Back then, my friends and I never used the term *break up*; we "quit" one another. And the objective was to quit your boo before your boo quit you. Otherwise, you'd have to constantly defend yourself to classmates as well as your ex: "You tryna quit me? I quit you first!" And so it went.

My gut was telling me that my J-O-B and I were at that point. We were too through—with each other. I was not long for this parenting babble. The tips and advice I was being asked to give out to readers had absolutely no relevance to everyday life. In fact, the information was more damaging than helpful because all it did was give mothers more crap to pile onto their already overwrought selves. Parenting sites and magazines were peddling the same kind of fare as women's service publications. It was a holier-than-thou, "let us tell you how you should be doing this" kind of attitude that exploited a mother's anxiety. How was the average mom elevated by a couple of chicks sitting up in Manhattan offices telling her how cool crappy two-hundred-dollar made-from-paper toys were?

Shortly after that assignment, I got another—from the same site, but from an editor who was a young mom to a toddler and infant. She wanted a piece on traveling with kids—by plane, by car—including "surprise, insider-type tips" that could make a mom's life easier. It should've been clear to me from the get-go that this would be a problematic way to make coin. When I filed the first draft, I quoted some airline communications person on the beauty of off-peak days and times. It wasn't exactly a Jack-in-the-box

kind of surprise tip. But I saw it in the category of "*A-ha . . .
I hadn't thought of that*"—stuff like avoid the weekends, if
possible, as well as Mondays, and opt for midday over early
morning, when business flyers would likely crowd the ter-
minals.

Her response? "This would be hard for most working
moms to do."

I thought, *Look, heifer. You asked for the* best *way to
fly with kids—not the easiest.* Was I being overly sensitive? To me, it sounded like old girl was coming for me—
passive-aggressively saying, "That off-peak business is
nice for someone like you freelancer, work-from-home-
type moms. But important people like me? Not so much."
I chirped back—and I know this probably came off badly
through e-mail—"last I checked, working moms get vacation and personal days." Then I added a smiley face. Two
can play passive-aggressive, missy.

I filed a revision, begrudgingly. I was worn out by this
time. Not because I was above such service pieces. I didn't
mind spouting tips. As you may have noticed, I humbly
consider myself a font of wisdom. It's just that with these
parenting pieces, I was done. All tipped out. Obviously I
was in no position to turn down work. But after writing
and editing so many of the same kinds of articles and with
three kids of my own at home—from toddler to tween—I
had just one tip for other mothers. And I wanted to shout

it from a bullhorn: There is no easy way to do anything with kids!

No formula. No diagram. No strategy. Mothering is hard, sometimes gut-wrenching even. And the only way to make it fairly simple is to find your own way to raise your kids—a way that won't make you lose your rabid mind.

That's it. The headline, the deck, the lead, and the body . . . end of article. No one wants to hear that, though. Instead, I get to trade e-mails with an editor who marks up my copy with inane comments that pass for edits. For example, I suggested in the third paragraph or so that moms give kids a little bitty treat to get them to sit quietly for a spell. But, I cautioned, too much sweets could send little ones off the rails. Fancy pants noted: "studies re: link btw sugar+hyper kids=inconclusive ☺ pls delete."

If I'm lying, I'm flying. She actually fixed her bony fingers to type those words. A real loony tune, that one. Okay, smart one. Let's wait for what studies say about candy sending kids off-the-rails crazy. Shudder to think we use an iota of common sense. But it wasn't her fault. She was doing her job. What did I expect? Hers was just one, in a striking series, of many wake-up calls smacking me upside my head lately.

Ignorance is never a good defense. But the truth is that for years I had unwittingly been doing the same dastardly deeds as this woefully misguided editor. I thought I was helping people. I know that sounds corny, but I took seriously my responsibility as a parenting journalist. Of course, there were aspects of the job that I didn't particularly like at times. Generally, though, I felt good about my career. Now, come to find out I was no better than the mommy marketers I looked down on.

Okay, I wasn't hawking anything as deleterious as "My Baby Can Read" kits. But my hands were not clean. Ever watch the evening news when a storm looms? The stations post reporters in every corner of town to gin up anxiety and speculate on what the storm *might* do to the roads, business owners, crops—you name it. Well, in a way, I was doing the same thing. No matter how well intended and wittily disguised, as a parenting editor I was finding potential problems—then offering up solutions wrapped in pithy prose.

These packaged tips and advice pieces were doing little to boost and empower moms. Quite the contrary, they were pimping moms' fears—hijacking their natural maternal instincts and getting them strung out on experts. If you take little ole me and multiply my editorial acumen (which is substantial, if I say so myself) by several thousand more journalists and bloggers—BAM! There you have it: a thriving industry built on manic mommyhood.

I thought to myself, I was just like Biggie. Maybe I wasn't big, black, and ugly as ever, however (no Gucci socks or watch filled with rocks). But guess what? I had to admit, "I'm not only a client, I'm a playa president . . ."

Game need change.

CHAPTER SIXTEEN

Go 'Head on—
Wit'cha Bad Self

Sugar was Mama's very best friend in the whole wide world. And, don't take this the wrong way, because Mama was—and is—a hoot to be around. But she won't let just anybody in. Her standards are very high. You know those Blow Pop suckers with bubble gum in the center? Mama was the opposite of that. To the outside world, she was easygoing, light, and bubble-licious. Her inside is where the hard candy lay hidden. Have you ever scraped your tongue or the roof of your mouth on the rough sticky coating of a lollipop?

It can present quite the conundrum—if you have a candy jones like I do. Despite the temporary sting a candy-splintered mouth presents, your taste buds demand that you keep licking and licking. Obviously, like any impairment, one could only remain capable and high functioning for so long. That's why, for me, Sugar ranked somewhere alongside Mother Teresa for her unflinching devotion to Mama. She had to be a saint, I reasoned. Someone who'd sooner lay down and die for Mama than display a tinge of anything that would even have the appearance of betrayal, indecency, disrespect, laziness, duplicity, or other human faults. Sugar was honey-dipped love and virtue through and through.

So it was fitting that she be called so. I was almost a teenager before I realized that Sugar was not her government name. She'd been christened Ellen. Nice enough, I guess, but altogether inadequate.

As her name would suggest, Sugar loved on my siblings and me *all* the time. I don't think she could have loved us more if we came from her own womb. Her children—practically grown when she entered our lives—were like aunts and uncles to us. Her ex-husband, Jack, was the trifling sort, from what I could gather, which may have cemented their bond, a relationship first born of convenience. Back in 1958, when Mama brought my big brother home from the hospital, it was Sugar—then, our upstairs neighbor—who helped her navigate all things baby. Sugar was a good fifteen years or so Mama's senior, so it would be easy to assume that she was this maternal elder type of figure. I don't think that was the case. They loved each other unconditionally the way a mother and daughter might. But the friendship was not weighted like that. Maybe on some level their souls joined because of that void in Mama's life. But they were more like peers than anything else. They teased and joked and cussed each other—with love. Much love. In fact, I never saw Mama love anyone the way she loved Sugar.

Through the two of them I learned what sisterhood looked like, what it sounded like, what it felt like: seeing them sharing their sillies on some days, trading support and sage counsel on others.

I'm certain that black women don't have a corner on strong friendship. We do, however, have our own particular ways of expressing it. You've heard the phrases, even if you didn't quite understand them. To outsiders they may sound like some kind of hackneyed urban-speak, but us black women are usually encouraged by this kind of talk. I can only speak for myself, but trust me when I utter these statements, I am really truly feeling love for a sister. For example:

- Uh-uh! Don't hurt nobody! (Translation: You got it going on.)
- All right. I see you now! (Translation: I like your swagger.)
- Handle your business! (Translation: You're doing your thing.)
- Do the dag-gone thing! (Translation: Same as above.)

- You ain't said nothing but a word! (Translation: I agree with you wholeheartedly.)
- Girl, you can do bad all by yourself! (Translation: That situation/person working your last nerve? Let that go.)

That's the way Mama and Sugar spoke to each other all the time. And although I was only privy to one side of the phone conversation—and those tidbits were to be taken in on the low, lest Mama accuse me of being all up in her mouth (translation: eavesdropping)—I got enough of the gist to understand what was really important. Women like Mama and Sugar were affirming one another. They were saying, "I know the world is not telling you this right now, but no matter what anybody says, you's a bad mama jamma!"

It was a girlfriend-to-girlfriend way of communicating strength and personal power—"Love yourself" and "Be your best self"—long before Oprah hit the airwaves. Underneath all those expressions, I was only now coming to realize the most potent message in the back-and-forth: "Be yourself even if that means you have to be *by* yourself." I was not going to be with the mom crowd. I was betwixt and between the stay-at-home and career set. I wasn't trying to obsess over my kids' test scores, enrichment activities, and athletic prowess. I didn't have enough money to join the town's exclusive country clubs. I didn't want to be defined by my address, my car, my husband, my Junior League participation, or the society circuit invites in my mailbox. And, most of all, I didn't have the time or energy to fake the funk.

From Mama and Sugar, I witnessed the way two women—devoted mothers, each with their share of challenges—loved on one other. They taught me that, first and foremost, you have to love on yourself. And that doing so was not an act of selfishness, but an act of strength and wisdom and fortitude. This modern habit of mothers, almost bragging that they've no time to take care *of* themselves, no time to care *for* themselves? It's not cute.

Unfortunately, in the prime of my mothering years, Sugar and I rarely got to spend the kind of lazy afternoons together that marked my childhood. She knew and loved my kids, of course. And she was thrilled to see me grow and mature as a mom. But more often than not, I was in Buffalo for only a weekend or so. And my visits with Sugar were reduced to drive-bys. I didn't take the time to sit at her feet and ask questions or seek her advice.

Once the crazy busyness of caring for toddlers had passed, seemingly out of nowhere, Sugar was diagnosed with Alzheimer's. She had to go into a nursing home. Her bright eyes grew more and more vacant, but the sweetness never left. Sugar always had a pleasant smile on her face as she greeted visitors. And Mama made sure she looked her best at all times—washing and pressing Sugar's clothes every week, brushing her hair, dressing her replete with nice earrings. Mostly, though, she talked to Sugar the way she always had—as though she weren't sick at all. And whether or not she knew what Mama was saying—or even who Mama was—she smiled, and sometimes even laughed.

As difficult as it was to see our Sugar slipping away, it was a blessing to see God's hand at work in our lives. Once Sugar as we'd always known her had irretrievably escaped my godmother's eyes, her daughter—and only surviving child, out of four—was diagnosed with pancreatic cancer. He spared Sugar the anguish that would've surely killed her. The rest of us had to face it, though. I still remember the wonder and sorrow in my girls' faces as I wailed out loud. If I couldn't see a life without these two important family members, I could only imagine Mama's grief— suffering the loss of her best friend and her best friend's "baby." She was a woman in her early sixties with grown daughters of her own, but still.

Losing them—and Beverly—took a while to come to terms with. I'd never really experienced death before. Well, that's not entirely true. Papa died many years ago. But I was only a kid, barely eight years old. At the time I mostly longed for his physical presence, which had shaped my early life in such a way that his absence in the day-to-

Go 'Head on—Wit'cha Bad Self

day activities of life left a huge void. For some reason, I most missed breakfast with Papa. I know that may seem strange. But that was our golden time of day, when we spent the most time just talking, just being together.

He would make me breakfast. Papa ignored the pot of grits Mama left on the stove before going to work, because I didn't like grits. I wanted Lucky Charms cereal. Thank you very much. Mama told him every day to be sure I had a hot breakfast. So each day Papa took loving care to warm the milk for my marshmallow hearts, clovers, and magical deliciousness. Then he'd pour himself a cup of coffee, fresh brewed from the stovetop percolator. I marveled at the ritual of it all. We had these white-and-gold-colored Corelle dishes at the time, which included what I regarded as fancy cup and saucer sets. Papa sat there as I drank the syrupy-sweet milk left over from my cereal. Mama was kind of proper about rules of eating and drinking. But Papa didn't mind if I took up the whole bowl and slurped myself silly. Once I was done, my attention inevitably turned to his coffee cup.

The way he sipped it in profound silence made me think that brew surely held some wondrous mysteries of the universe. And I was desperate for a li'l taste. Papa, so bemused by my daily begging routine, would hold out for as long as possible. He tried every tool of dissuasion he could think of: "Your mama won't like it." "It's too strong for you."

241

"You don't want none of this." After I kept at him for a while—he sometimes said I was the "beggingest child" he'd ever seen—Papa would look at me in a sad attempt to be stern with his most dire warning yet: "You know, coffee will make you black," as if to say, *Are you sure about this?*

"Good, Imma be black as you, Papa!" I'd squeal. A broad smile would take over his entire cocoa-brown face as he poured me my own spot of joe, heavily mixed with Pet evaporated milk. Once I got my way, I'd drink quietly—attempting to mimic Papa's pensive sips. I loved the stoicism he displayed. I cannot recall him ever raising his voice. He appeared quite bothered at times during the evening news, especially for some reason, when Richard Nixon was speaking. But he'd just sigh, mostly, as the old Cronkite guy talked about Vietcong and death and soldiers and such. I had no real idea what the news was about. And Papa never let on how upset he was by the news, in the same way that he never spoke ill of my dad, whose behavior had to make his blood boil. I would learn much later that Papa was my bridge over troubled waters. Because of him, I never sensed any discord in my life whatsoever. He taught us optimism and honor and faith. Like Mama, he also believed strongly that you just keep on keeping on in life. No matter what. But if Mama was aged Scotch, one hundred proof, Papa was a lightly flavored wine cooler. Any hiccup or disappointment, he reckoned, could be turned around with a sunny attitude. "One monkey don't stop no show," he'd laugh.

Other than Richard Nixon's speeches on the news and Dad's bombastic visits, few things ruffled Papa's feathers. I'm sure he never believed that Dad had met any of the celebrities he spoke of. Not B. B. King or Bobby Blue Bland. Not the Mighty Clouds of Joy or the Dixie Hummingbirds. And definitely not the Queen of Soul. Papa never had a disparaging word for anyone, but his silence always spoke volumes. *Still water run deep . . . Yes, it do.*

The deaths of the formidable matriarchs in my life left a different kind of longing—a thirst for soul and depth and meaning. Their absences, the loss of their fullness and wholeness, put a strobe light shine on my empty parts. Those areas in my life that I'd thought were filled up were really just busy. I was doing many, many things. It was obvious from the dry-erase calendar prominently featured in my kitchen, with bulletin board and magnetized notepad attached. My family, like every other family I knew, had places to go and things to do. All. The. Time.

All the doing left scant time for *being*. A lot of times, I didn't feel like a mother so much as I felt like the sum of my to-do list. Lucky for me, many of my duties led me to cross paths with a few really cool women. Each of my kids has at least a couple of friends whose mothers I love and adore, women I'd hang out with even if it weren't convenient. But outside our kids I seldom made time for those relationships. Instead, I contented myself with impromptu chats on the sidelines of a soccer game or quick exchanges at drop-off or pickup times.

Obviously times have changed. Kids don't go outside and just play as we did growing up—although on occasion I have locked my kids outside, just on General Principle but I usually give in once they start crying really, really loudly. I am not likely to see the day when I sit down in the kitchen on the phone with a cigarette and gossip with girl-friends. For starters, I don't smoke. And, besides, that's why God invented cell phones and outdoor decks.

It was clear to me that all the important women in my life would've said the same thing, in unison, had they caught a glimpse of my so-called life: "Will you just go someplace and sit down?" I began to realize that if I was going to honor the strong black women in my life, I had to first honor me.

CHAPTER SEVENTEEN

What We 'Bout to Do Right Here Is Go Back

When you grow up in a town perennially on the come-up, it's the attractions other cities take for granted that stand out and create excitement. Once the steel mills and virtually every manufacturer in our backyard began to get out of Dodge in the 1970s, city officials were forever promising that Buffalo, the "Queen City" (trust me, the irony of that nickname is not lost on its citizenry), would become a leader in banking. Then there was the big savings and loan crisis with Wonder Woman's husband. Then we were going to be a hub for tourism, I think. That didn't work out so well either. It became clear to me early on that Buffalo was like the Evans family of *Good Times* fame. As James said often, "Florida, I swear to God. If it wasn't for bad luck, we wouldn't have no luck at all."

Probably that's why Dad tried so hard to keep his player card full. Although he and I never shared a real closeness,

I always knew he loved my siblings and me. I am grateful for his buoyant spirit. Certainly no one ever showed him what a warm hug and heart-to-heart conversation could do. But he did his best, in the language he knew, to make his kids happy. And he did a pretty good job. Because of him, I don't have sense enough to understand "my place." I've always been comfortable anywhere. When I moved to New York, I used to sometimes take myself to places like the Plaza and the St. Regis Hotel. Guess I got some game from my daddy. Of course, I could only afford coffee. But fancy places like that bring you a few cookies alongside the java, making the thirteen-dollar expenditure quite a value when you think about it. I did it only occasionally. But I enjoyed sipping from fancy bone china. And the cookies? Like butta, baby! My friends thought I was crazy. They didn't get what I found so special about sitting up in gilded lobbies people-watching and such. Pity.

Mama had a bit of baller in her too. Hers was just more balanced. We didn't go out just to be going somewhere. We took in what really mattered to her—Isaac Hayes, James Brown concerts, and plays—usually by bus. Sometimes they were the traveling productions of genuine, legit Broadway shows; other times, locally produced performances at Buffalo's own Ujima Theater—which, I believe, still stands. Mama didn't skimp on culture.

None of this compared to the highlight of our family's

social calendar: the Ebony Fashion Fair show. It all went down at Kleinhans Music Hall—the swankest venue in town and home to the Buffalo Philharmonic Orchestra. The circular architecture was unlike anything else in Buffalo, kind of like our version of New York's Guggenheim—though not quite as grand or remarkable or famous. Still, it was ours. And it was a big deal. I didn't know it then, but apparently the Ebony Fashion Fair was sponsored by The Links Incorporated—which explains why it was high post. The Links is a very exclusive black organization whose membership eligibility is tied to certain income requirements. You have to make well over two hundred thousand dollars or so, I think. In Buffalo that kind of cheddar was akin to millionaire status—whether you were black, white, or purple. I was totally oblivious to status levels when I was growing up. I guess I figured if anyone was all that, why did they live in the same dingy town as the rest of us?

It never dawned on me that some people in my town traveled in highfalutin circles. I knew of high class—or low class, for that matter—only peripherally. I'd heard, and even used, the term *bourgeois*, but I thought it referred to people with fancy mannerisms, like holding your glass with a pinkie finger extended. I also had a set of friends who were involved in another upper-middle-class club for black people—Jack and Jill. I can't recall how or when, but it was made clear to me that it was a club for fancy kids.

The kids didn't seem all that different from me, although I did note that they all had bigger homes in areas of Buffalo I wasn't all that familiar with. I was totally unfazed. I thought, "Why would anyone want to be part of a club named after Mother Goose characters?" It all just seemed silly to me.

As a child of Mama's, though, I knew good clothes and good style. When we went to expensive stores, she took the time to explain things like fabric, cut, and facing. These were very fine threads at the Ebony Fashion Fair. The black people of Buffalo turned it *out*. Mama herself was no slouch—with her sheath dresses and foxtails (borrowed, I'm guessing). She wore clothes well. Like Dad, she was tall, thin, and strikingly attractive. I'm not sure which fashion show delighted more—the one onstage or the one displayed during intermission. Mama seemed to know some of these folks; I'm not sure how. Or maybe everybody was just friendly and hospitable, seeing as how Buffalo was so rarely treated to such international attractions.

You have to understand, for most Buffalo consumers, "designer" clothes meant Calvin Klein jeans and Liz Claiborne blazers. In the words of Oran "Juice" Jones, the Ebony Fashion Fair exposed us hicks to "things we couldn't even pronounce." This stylish spectacle was a hugely big deal. Buffalo's black population was not large; it's historically been predominantly Polish (factoid: Martha Stewart has roots in my city, as does actress Vanessa Williams). We loved to witness the all-black production—if there were white folks present, I didn't notice—especially the famous models we got to know on a first-name basis. And talk about "Sashay, Shanté!" Seeing the languid gorgeousness of black women strutting their stuff on the catwalk, you could almost feel the bass keep time with their hips—like, "uh!" This was the closest any of us came to Paris or even Manhattan, for that matter. The emcee of the evening was always in ultradramatic form—enunciating every syllable with flourish. I'd never in my young life heard a black person speak with such authority and power.

Years later, when I ended up at Northwestern University near Chicago, I liked to tell people I was drawn to the well-known journalism program. That was only half true. Back when I'd heard that emcee from the Ebony Fashion Fair shows announce, *Chi-caaaa-go!* in that sexy, exaggerated exultation, I think it was indelibly seared in my brain. "The Chi" had an allure that was for me exotic and familiar at the same time. The blackness of the South Side seemed to me all that Buffalo could have been. Only if. The people were down-home and simple (in a good way) and it had soul—not just as home to Curtis Mayfield and Chaka Khan, it was a place you could feel.

Style was important in Chicago—although it wasn't always a style the rest of the country would relate to.

Whether or not you could appreciate the average Chicagoan's penchant for bright colors and carefully matched ensembles, one thing was clear. A sister's do had to be done up right. Chi-town women were all about the hairstyle. I think even if you were dead broke there was no acceptable excuse for a raggedy head. My friends and I traveled to Chicago from Northwestern University's campus in suburban Evanston for the best stylists around. And this was on paltry college-student budgets. We didn't go often, but—almost like our educations—the right haircut was an investment.

I had all kinds of looks back then: bangs, bobs, asymmetrical shags, cellophane highlights, you name it. Hair was critically important. When I moved to New York City, I was surprised to note the many braided extensions and jacked-up weaves. A proper 'do was not the hallowed topper to which I'd become accustomed. Sisters in Gotham unabashedly sported dry, overprocessed hair—the likes of frayed ends, edges that were tattered to near-barren, and (this one really shocked me) stiff, heavily oiled curls. I followed my black girl instincts and made appointments at all the top salons, like Black Hair Is, which I'd seen written up in major black magazines—to no avail. I was greeted by greasy sheen–spraying armies of stylists. Their own do's were major don'ts. And many of them slathered Revlon Extra-Strength Relaxer on my hair from root to tip—which was the first step on the road to ruin chemically processed hair.

I am nothing if not resourceful, though. So I didn't give up, and I didn't submit to the standard-issue braid-extension styles of the day. Not that anything is wrong with the whole Nefertiti look. It just wasn't quite me. More important, I didn't need Madame C.J. Walker to resurrect and pull my coat to the fact that all that tightness along my edges would not be a good look over time. Instead, I placed a cold call to the Vidal Sassoon salon—located, at the time, on Fifth Avenue in the then General Motors Plaza. Point-blank, I asked, "Does anyone there do black hair?" I was given two names. I couldn't pronounce the one that sounded Southeast Asian. So I booked a session with Penny—who I learned on the day of my appointment was also Asian. In my head, I was picturing Janet Jackson's character from *Good Times*. But no worries. What did I have to lose? Penny and I talked—well mostly, she talked about how I needed a haircut to accommodate my large and sloping forehead. I knew about the large part. My brother and sister called me "five-head" for most of my life. The sloping thing was new to me, but when she swung me around in her chair with mirrors on all sides, I pretty much got what she meant.

First, though, I would have a touch-up with the "chemical" person. Coming toward me was a freakishly tall black

man with blue platform shoes and dreadlocks that appeared to grow out of his head and straight to the sky—
defying the laws of gravity in dramatic fashion. Sherwin
had big, brown eyes and lovely lashes—sort of like a black
male Kewpie doll. I decided then and there he would be
my hair boo forever. We talked about everything and
nothing—all in a shorthand that we both quickly deci-
phered. We laughed when we looked at each other, for reasons I don't think either of us understood. Turns out,
Sherwin was also fairly new to the Big City, having moved
from—you guessed it—Chicago. We had all the same cultural references: classic R&B, house music, and Southern
sayings like, "Imma tell you one mo' 'gain," which never
failed to slay us both.

That was more than twenty-some-odd years ago. I actually have the "some-odd" figure precisely committed to
memory. But I can't tell it on account of Sherwin might
not appreciate me putting his business in the street. If you
have jumped to the conclusion that Sherwin and I have
a typical client-hairdresser relationship, you would be
wrong. I mean, I love him dearly and he carries deep and
abiding affection for me. But we are not really confidants
per se. We don't talk about our relationships. We don't
even gossip—unless you count the stuff we both learn
from Wendy Williams. I don't need to tell him my secrets,
because he just knows. Seriously, somehow, Sherwin intu-

its exactly where I am in my life and what I need to take me, hairwise and otherwise, through that moment.

I don't think I have ever told Sherwin what to do with my hair. I never bring magazine clippings or go through lengthy descriptions. As a matter of professional course, he asks me—as he does all of his clients—"What are we doing today?" And my response is usually, "You already know." Then we crack up. Sometimes we sing songs—old ones, naturally—spontaneously. Years ago, I told him— and I remind him to this day—that though New York real estate, boyfriends, and jobs may change, he can't leave me. Ever. That usually prompts us to break out in Jennifer Holliday—or J Hud, if you prefer—rendition of "I'm Staying" (*and you're gonna love me!*). Or it could be that house track "It's Not Over" (*even the stars declare that you belong to me!*). Either is appropriate and neither of us has a problem acting a fool. I think, between you and me, Sherwin has me beat in the fool department. Just saying. He has a necklace he wears in public that tells the world to back off him, in fact. He long ago retired his blue platform shoes, trading them in for a tight sneaker game. His locks are gone now too. He'd been paring them back for years. First for an errant afro that led every other passerby in downtown Manhattan to mistake him for that cutie-pie soul crooner Maxwell—which Sherwin found a bit irritating. Then he moved to his current style. It is his own invention made whole by a combination of petrified kinks—he seldom combs it—and water. He is a genius of color, mixing and matching dyes and ammonia to correct bleached blonds, bring boldness to brunettes, and add sparks to redheads. Maybe all that chemical perfecting inclines him to let his own hair simply do what it do.

I realize it sounds crazy, but the messy coif thing works. Probably because Sherwin is so fine. Good-looking men can pull off that no-maintenance look in a way that women just can't. Between the dimples, the eyes, his tall, thin frame, and that devilish grin, perfect hair might make Sherwin unapproachable. I've watched him work on his clients—wealthy-looking professional women (Gloria Steinem has sat in his chair), young hipsters (especially in media), distinguished men. He can talk about anything with them. Politics. Football, which he loooves. Travel. History.

He and I just goof around, like brother and sister—he being the older one, of course.

On some occasions, we don't actually sing. We just speak the lyrics and add our own flourishes. Out of nowhere, we recently both channeled Bobby Womack—at the same time. He'd gone into the back room to measure and mix my color application. Upon his return, he grinned. "Miss me?" I nodded, then it just took on a life of its own.

Sherwin: You think you lonely now, don't you?

Me: Honey, you betta wait until to*night!*

Then, when both our stomachs were hurting from laughing so much, I managed to say: "Always be complaining about me never being at home . . ." Then together, we wailed: "I can't be in two places at one tiiiiime!" He called his mom in Chicago after our little duet and I explained that her child was crazy, but I loved him. We kept laughing after that—so hard that everyone in the salon, maybe in the world, would be convinced we were on drugs. I'm actually laugh-crying in this very moment. *Oooh wee!* I just love me some Sherwin—like slow-cooked food.

Since the mid-nineties, I'd rocked natural hair. I'm not trying to brag on myself or anything. That, like, I got it going on. That's not for me to say (if you say it, I ain't finna argue). But I was happy to be nappy long before it was discovered in the blogosphere and every sister with some gel and a headband replaced the word *kinky* with "texture." Over a fifteen-year period I had a short, cropped 'fro. I had a long, curly 'fro. I had a blond 'fro. And I had every iteration of 'fro in between. It was my look—the only look my kids had ever seen, in fact.

A couple of years ago, I made my quarterly booking with Sherwin and Penny. (I may have forgotten to mention that lavishing my locks cost me dearly. Since I be balling on a budget, I have never been what you would call a frequent salon visitor.) As usual, I had no particular agenda in mind. I figured Penny would shape me up and Sherwin would give me some fresh highlights or some such.

This was an appointment I sorely needed. Not because my hair was badly in need of a tune-up. It was. But more importantly, I needed a tune-up. It was an exciting year for me, in many respects. Each of my kids was set to embark on a brand-new season in life. Cole would soon enter kindergarten (good-bye preschool tuition). Trinity was beginning middle school. And Chloe was ready to start high school. Oh, and me? Well, I hadn't graduated to anything at all—except the realization that I had finally had three kids who required a lot less of me. And the rest of me had made no real plans for this new level of freedom. I needed Sherwin to make me laugh. To share some new, exciting adventure he'd undertaken.

He rarely disappointed in this department. Over the years, Sherwin had regaled me with crazy stories of parachute jumps, zip-lining, and Burning Man desert treks. Even his relatively mundane exploits entertained. He somehow got to see a modern-day live performance with Grace Jones and a small-venue serenade with Patti LaBelle. And he was the only black person I knew who'd ever gone to one of those participatory dinner theaters. You know, the kind where everyone assumes a character and has to solve a mystery of some sort?

Sherwin lived and I wanted to hear about his life, because mine was pretty dull. When I sat down in his chair, he began with: "Ylonda. Ylonda. Ylonda." Three times, with a deep breath at the end. As I faced the mirror, he too faced the mirror. And looked straight ahead, deadpan as though he were setting up a joke, but none came.

Staring deep at my reflection, he touched my 'fro and unapologetically said: "I'm over this, aren't you?" I'm not sure what I was supposed to say. How long had he found my look so uninspired? So tired? Of course, I'd been struggling myself to understand where my sexy had gone. Surely it got up and went at some point over the past few years. Exactly when, I didn't know. And, certainly, if I'd known where, I'd have run after it. Sherwin was right. This *Motherland* reminder no longer suited me. I figured he would suggest I go blond again or maybe cut the 'fro really short. That could be cute. Right?

Now that he was confident that he'd won me over to his way of thinking, a mischievous grin broke across Sherwin's face. Did I mention his dimples? He did a little happy dance in place and made a pronouncement thusly: "What we 'bout to do right now is go back—waaay back." I laughed—always a sucker for something crazy like Jimmy Castor—but still I had no idea of his plan. At this point, you might conclude that I am enormously trusting or enormously stupid. I'm not sure which myself. I'll spare you all the chemical details.

But, trust that I walked out of that Manhattan salon feeling lighter, and hotter, than I'd felt in a long, long time. My hair was fried, lyed, and laid to the side in a re-laxed pixie style. Penny hooked it up so that, depending on how I moved my head, my hair hung over one eye in a coquettish smolder. It was FIYAH (like Wendy used to say on the radio). So much so that I just had to linger awhile at the Chelsea-area street vendors for new earrings and sunglasses—although the sun had already started to set. Beauty doesn't need to be practical. It only has to look good. And the hotness going on atop my head convinced me that pending dusk or no, my future was so bright I needed shades.

I walked the twenty blocks uptown to the Port Author-ity Bus Terminal and alighted (Note: Before my new 'do, I simply took a seat on the bus; my new look was cause to alight). In my head, I was singing Patti LaBelle and imag-ining Sherwin on backup: *"Ooh, ooh, ooh, ooh, ooooob . . . I got a new attitude!"* When I walked in the house, the whole family was dumbstruck. Not a one of them had ever seen me so fresh and so clean-clean. I'd been au naturel, nature girl their entire lives. It would take Cole to speak for ev-eryone, to put words to what everyone else felt but could not articulate. My baby burst out with a joyful smile, ran up to my arms, and said: "Mommy, why do you look like somebody I do not know?"

CHAPTER EIGHTEEN

Act Like You Got
Some Sense

I think I get it now. Finally.

Between Mama's teachings in my past and looking ahead—really looking—into my kids' future, I was beginning to see the present more clearly. Unbeknownst to me, it had been jacked up for a minute. With nothing but loving intentions, out of some warped sense of obligation and circumstantial confusion, I had been lying like a mug. To myself.

It was time to strip life down . . . to put the *life* back in *family life*. I'm not sure what I'd been waiting for all this time. But it was high time for me to be the change I wanted to see—to borrow a campaign slogan. It's hard to explain, but it meant starting with a lot of little things. For example, my kids were mildly interested in music. Did that really mean we needed weekly piano lessons in the Suzuki method? In a lightbulb moment, I said to myself: "Guess what? If God had designed your children to be musical prodigies, he'd likely have given you a sign by now." I sat down with my morning coffee one day and I got a James Brown revelation right then and there. I never asked for it. The wisdom just fell in my lap and I thought, "Girl, you gotta give it up and turn it loose." I was proud and I know the Godfather of Soul would be pleased as well.

Sherwin, in his own inimitable way, had lit a fire under me. You know that place in the record when the DJ says, "Rewind that back"? Yeah, that. No, we couldn't go back to rabbit-ear antennae and Applejack hats, but there was plenty of room to add some little classic soul into the mix.

While Mama was nowhere near nursing home eligible, she was slowing. And, as she did so, I felt the air of mortality blowing like a Smokey Robinson "Quiet Storm." She came to visit recently to see my younger daughter star in her school play. I have been forever vexed by Mama's near-maniacal insistence that things *look* right. That we *act* right. That we *talk* right. It is all starting to make sense. As a kid, I naturally presumed she was just tripping. I thought, how important could it possibly be that we dress neatly all the time. I mean, sometimes you just don't feel like stressing over ironed, matching clothes. Right?

Yet, even now, Mama steps out looking as fly as any septuagenarian possibly could. Mind you, old girl's feet are all tore up, ravaged by arthritis, hammertoe, and all manner of painful and inconvenient senior ailments. She should really want to rock those thick-bottomed orthopedics 24/7. But no. That's not even happening.

I have come to take Mama's seeming vanities for granted. I barely noticed Mama strut into the elementary school multipurpose room wearing a red belted dress and high-heeled slingbacks. But when she came to Trinity's play, my girlfriend—Carmen Jackson—was outdone. "No, your mama didn't just walk up in here giving us waist! Girl, women our age can't *even*! I'm scared. Okay? I am scared right now. Your mama ain't playing." I love Carmen because she is the realest. I had to stop and think about it. But she was right. Who rolls like that? Nobody but Mama.

I could've asked why but I already knew. The reason for her turning it out for a 10:30 A.M. curtain call? Mama always told us: "If you look like shit, people will treat you like shit."

She long ago decided no one would treat her like, well— you know, ever again.

She'd had enough of that business growing up. Mama doesn't like to talk about her childhood. And what my siblings and I do know, we've sort of had to piece together from snippets Mama dropped over the years and our extended family members. After her biological mother passed on, Papa remarried. Big Mama (I swear I have never known her name) came into the marriage with her own set of kids.

Come to think of it, I guess she had two sets of kids from a couple of baby daddies, because the eldest was black to the level of bluelike purple and the others were a sort of vanilla latte color, with "good" hair—traits of which they were very proud, I think. I will always remember Mama's one stepsister, Aunt Lucille, coming by our house back in the day. As was customary, we kids were expected to serve guests. When Aunt 'Cille requested coffee, she would announce with a self-satisfied smirk—"Keep pouring that milk, baby. I want my coffee light like me!" I knew how she took it, but Aunt 'Cille never tired of reminding us of her complexion each time she came over. That's how it was back then. People wore their high-yellowness like a badge of honor.

It was never clear to me who was the daddy of Mama's beige stepsiblings, but Papa supported them on a rail worker's salary—a decent living for colored folks in the 1940s. His work meant lots of travel. And when he left town, Big Mama was savagely cruel—not only toward Mama, but toward my uncle Dave (who eventually ran away). Often, Mama got no food to eat. As a general rule, she was not allowed clothes or shoes until Big Mama's own children outgrew theirs to pass down to her. As a consequence to any behavior she disliked, Mama was forced to sleep outside.

Far worse than the physical mistreatment, Big Mama

was determined to break her unwanted stepchild—to crush her spirit. She taunted Mama daily by calling her "black and ugly." She told her she was dumb and would never amount to anything. Mama, a child herself, had no defenses. She always suspected that Papa knew about the abuse even though he wasn't present to witness it. She told us that when his job brought him back home, he would love on her as best he could. He'd buy her gifts and toys, but only felt comfortable lavishing her in private.

That wasn't going to cut it. Mama would stubbornly refuse Papa and insist, "If you can't give it to me in front of her, I don't want it." But Big Mama lorded over Papa as well. She'd shot him once. Mama's three sisters hightailed it out of Birmingham and went to live in Mississippi, where family on my maternal grandmother's side lived.

From the few photos I've seen, Big Mama bore a striking resemblance to Notorious B.I.G. In a woman, that was not cute. Probably she was bothered by Mama's high cheekbones and chiseled good looks. So poisoned by self-hate, she couldn't have liked the fact that Mama's regal nose and other features were in stark contrast to her coarse ones. Her claim to fame, I guess, was lying with some white or near-white man to produce fair-skinned children. Obviously she was disturbed beyond reasoning. Pixilated (country-speak for "crazy"). She stole stuff from neighbors and planted the ill-begotten goods on Mama. Word is when Big Mama finally died and went home to be with the devil, wedding rings, cash, and myriad other valuables were found among her personal effects—all items she'd lifted and framed Mama for.

Mere mortals would've caved under such tyranny. More than five decades later, my uncle Dave could still hear Big Mama's torment in his head. In fairness, his diabolical stepmother was not the only voice; he struggled against a mix of demons, including substance abuse and mental illness. His wretched memories of the past surely didn't comfort him when he took that Smith & Wesson to his temple some years back.

Through a mix of God's grace and indomitable grit, Mama decided early on that she would not be bowed. She says rather than cry, she willed herself to stand with steely resolve in the face of evil. She had a mantra too: "I'll show her."

It remains paramount to Mama that you "show" people—show them what you're worth, she'd say. Show people how to treat you. Critical to this piece is your comportment. The vagaries of old age have weighed in over the past few years, but if you ask anyone who has met Mama what makes her special, they will tell you that hands-down it is her walk.

Mama walks like she is the Queen of Sheba. As a child I was equal parts awed and mortified by her stride. I am sure when the very first catty woman on earth looked at her very first catty girlfriend and said, "Who the hell does she think she is?" they were looking at Mama and watching that walk. Her back and shoulders were so upright, at first glimpse it could appear that something—a stick, a pole—might be stuck up Mama's behind. But not everything surrounding her slight torso is washboard stiff. As her back pointed north, Mama's narrow hips slammed from east to west. Her alleged hips—they are extremely narrow—have this peculiar way of jutting in a fashion some would call "switching," but really it is far more powerful than that. If a soundtrack were playing when she sashayed from one point to the other, the bass line would go deep and low and the lead vocalist would have to say, "Uh!" each time she put one foot in front of the other.

As well as she walks the walk, Mama made it her business to talk the talk—to the best of her ability, at least. Diction for any southerner is a challenge. I'm just going to put this out there: Mama is as country as they come. And, remember, she grew up in Birmingham's segregated school system. College was never a consideration. Her first priority was getting the hell outta Dodge. She may not have all the grammar rules committed to memory. And her English is definitely not always the queen's. But Mama never let that stop her from speaking properly. And she would chide us if we failed to do the same.

If we said, "Where are my sneakers at?" you could bet that Mama's response would be a stern glare and "Look behind that preposition." As with most country people, certain words gave Mama a hard way to go: *Argue* seemed to turn into *argar.* In her rendition of the ABC song, the letter *R* had two syllables instead of one. And in written form, it was common for her to misjudge the juxtaposition of double vowels. She sometimes spelled "should" as "shuold."

None of those locution deficits, though, diminished Mama's sense of class. In fact, even when she was wrong, Mama had a way of carrying herself so highly you might think for a moment that *you* got the words wrong. She has always held tight to high standards of decorum and sophistication.

Never again would Big Mama, or anyone, assign her to the ranks of worthless good-for-nothings. With her hair laid, her clothes pressed, she'd put that backfield in motion and let the world know she was not to be played cheap.

And maybe if she worked assiduously at her Classy Lady skills—I'm talking day and night—just maybe those efforts could make Mama forget the depravity of her girlhood. Focusing on the proper fork to use, and when, just might erase the fact that she was denied food by someone charged with her care. Being clean and neat and pretty today could, perhaps, dull the sting of being treated like crap yesteryear.

Never having been mothered herself, Mama didn't have a whole lot in her toolbox. So she tried to give us what had worked for her. In her mind, I suppose if you *act* all right, things will *be* all right.

Growing up, when my siblings and I got crazy rambunctious, Mama was quick to yell: "You better act like you got some sense!" She meant for us to compose ourselves . . . to get some control of the situation. I'm certain she didn't anticipate the need for such admonitions once we became grown-ups. And if she was in any way displeased with the way my life had turned out, she never let on.

The irony is whether or not she knew I was half-stepping, in good conscience I couldn't get down like this. Starting now, Imma act like I got some sense—good sense.

CHAPTER NINETEEN

Reunited 'Cause
We Understood

Cole is only six years old. So it had to be just a short while ago when, as a baby, Mama would visit and push her grandson all over town in my jog stroller. Ambitious and sure-footed, Mama conquered the hilly, sloping avenues from our house to Starbucks and back again. No sweat. No strain. During her stays, my friends marveled at her energy. It was as though she were that Eyewitness News van, showing up everywhere—parks, schoolyards, you name it.

Over the past few years, all that's changed. Old age has begun nipping at Mama's heels, slowing her steps and rocking her stance. Years of physical toil have, I guess, taken their toll. As Mama and Sugar used to jokingly say, those two no-count brothers, Arthur and Ritis, were acting out and hurting something terrible. If I hadn't witnessed its ravages with my own two eyes, I'd never believe arthritis could be so debilitating. Mama falls and when she does so, she can't easily get up. The daily lives of my brother and sister, who still live in Buffalo, now include detours to allow for increased caregiving tasks. Not just Mama, but Dad too—who, interestingly enough, is in pretty good physical shape but wavers in and out of states of confusion. His stories, which always played fast and loose with facts, still sustain him. It took a while for me to understand that I should just play along. So when he talks about the time Oprah Winfrey and I were together in a magazine, I no longer say: "No, Dad. I wrote a freelance piece, and she was on the cover. We're not friends, Oprah Winfrey and me." He's an old man now—entitled to his grand fantasies.

I simply listen to his sometimes-rambling fantasies by phone. My sister and brother are the ones who actually see to it that his basic needs are met. Dad and the pious homewrecker are still "roommates." But if Dad's mental capacities get a little trippy on occasion, hers have left the building. All that lying, I imagine, messed up their heads. My brother reports, sadly, that her children—two daughters—rarely come around to check on her. I think they fell out with one another some time ago and each is, perhaps, waiting for the other to take the lead.

Dad and his younger brother, Mac, are the only surviving members of his family of five brothers and sisters. And although they don't visit all that often, many of my cousins on his side love and adore him. Most recall fondly his gregarious personality and sense of style. Probably he was the Gault family's original Mack Daddy. I won't speak for my brother and sister, but while there is not the slightest trace of bad blood, I never really felt a super-strong connection to the Gaults. I never knew Dad's father, who died years before I was born. As kids, we visited his mother relatively often, always on Christmas and other major holidays. Dad would cheerfully say, "Let's go to 59 Edna." Only just now has it dawned on me, the strangeness of calling Grandma's home by its street address.

I certainly didn't mind going there. We all ran around the house, ate sweets and such. It's just that Grandma had a whole bunch of grandchildren. And most came before me. I have cousins who are in their sixties. Not to say that's a terribly old age, but as a kid there really isn't much to chat about with cousins already in high school and college. By the time I came along, with a handful of other cousins of my generation, the thrill of grandkids may have begun to get old for her. She probably loved me in some fashion. I was polite enough. Cute enough; in fact, she often complimented my sister and me on our looks— how we were prettier than such-and-such cousin and with longer, better hair than so-and-so. Strange talk that made us chuckle nervously. Still, I never got that I was special to her. One year she got all the granddaughters the same jewelry box; all the grandsons got something boyish. It was a nice gesture, and probably very expensive, because I swear she had to have fifty grandchildren.

Here's the main thing, though. I had a sneaking suspicion that some of the Gaults, maybe Grandma included, were not Mama's biggest fans. I never heard anyone speak ill of her outright. Just a vibe. Dad—so dramatic with his tall tales—probably had them thinking Mama had, one day out of nowhere, just left him out in the cold. She did, actually. But that was only after he'd used up all of his chances.

Mama didn't come to Grandma's house with us all that often. On holidays, especially, she was tired after working to shop, assemble toys, cook, and all that stuff that Dad just showed up to enjoy. Grandma's house was pleasant. My aunt Dot, the only Gault who seemed to be a really good friend to Mama, took very good care to make 59 Edna a festive place to be. I will never forget the way she painstakingly took brown paint to the faces of all the Christmas angels and Santas that decorated the living room. Grandma was healthy as an ox from what I could tell—a big, strong, and beautiful woman of about six foot two with smooth skin and glistening eyes. She wore a mysterious smile as she sat in her chair or up in her bed, not doing or saying all that much. For me, the highlight of visits came when (and if) Grandma let down her hair. She had the longest, waviest starch-white hair that you could ever imagine. Usually, especially for church each Sunday, she wore it in a single braid wrapped around her head— Greek goddess style. Maybe that Aphrodite-like hairdo was a subconscious commentary on her life. Grandma— whose graceful charms trace back to her girlhood—was certainly loved and adored, it seemed. No one has come out and said she had affairs or anything, But she did up and leave her husband, traveling to a couple of cities before settling in Buffalo. Legend has it that she and a certain well-known Buffalo clergyman kept company, as they say. I have no earthly idea whether Grandma was running to the arms of another man or running away from the one she'd married. I do know, though, she abandoned my dad and his siblings—the youngest, only a toddler at the time. Still, my dad and my aunts and uncles seemed to worship the ground she walked on—if and when she got up to walk, of course. "Mother, would you like this?" "Mother, do you need that?" They all lavished her with attention and care, waiting on her hand and foot although she was strong and able-bodied. I never saw her step foot near the stove. In fact, I swear I never saw her get up to get or do anything—except go to church. So suffice it to say I never got any of that "Grandma's Hands" kind of cobbler-baking, jam-making love Bill Withers sang about. But so be it. When she died in the late 1980s she was close to a hundred years old.

Sometimes Dad tells stories about Grandma. Funny things she'd said or done. But I'd sooner believe his tales about celebrity sightings than accept his warm, comical memories of his mother. I mean, maybe they shared some intimacies no one saw. I never witnessed much of anything witty or remarkably endearing between them.

One thing is for sure: If Dad grows farther and farther from his reality as he ages, it's as though Mama is spending her golden years consumed with making peace with hers—exploring her truth, including the pains of her past. She recently began visiting her blood siblings in Macon, Mississippi, for the first time ever. And five years ago, when one of her older sisters was diagnosed with cancer, they knitted a closeness that fate had denied them as little girls in Birmingham. Aunt Francis fought toe-to-toe with that devil of a disease, as it traveled to her stomach and eventually her liver. That soldier spirit is apparently in our DNA, because—to hear Mama's reports—Aunt Francis was whipping cancer's butt and taking names. They talked on the phone often. And Mama trekked to Macon to nurse her sister as often as she could.

When Aunt Francis died, Mama's newly formed ties with her family survived—thrived, even. Her conversations became dotted with the names of relative strangers cum nieces, nephews, and cousins now in Macon as well as places like St. Louis and Flint. "So-and-so is getting married." "What's-his-face graduated college." Mama would talk about her folks as though we'd known them our whole lives. I didn't have the heart to tell her that Bobbie, Pat, and her namesake li'l Essie pretty much all melded together for me. I couldn't keep straight who lived where, who was whose son or daughter, or who was on first. While it was obvious that these rekindled relationships meant a lot to her, Mama still had few answers. And selfishly, I was still hung up on why as a four-year-old baby my mama was left behind in the first place. It didn't seem like any of that had been acknowledged—not even when Uncle Dave committed suicide.

A surprising but not altogether shocking turn of events. I barely knew Papa's namesake and Mama's only brother... didn't even lay eyes on him till the late eighties, when he mysteriously showed up at our doorstep in Buffalo. Even through the gray, gauzy haze of our screen door, I knew he belonged to us. I felt like I was staring into Papa's face. Mama had not seen him in nearly thirty years. She said the last she'd even heard from him was back when she and Dad married. As newlyweds, they'd passed through Georgia on a vacation and by phone, Uncle Dave had agreed to come to the hotel for a brief visit. As far as Mama knew, he was a no-show. But actually Uncle Dave *had* stopped by.

Problem was, he didn't know Mama's new married name.
And when he asked around for a woman named Essie, the
hotel manager thought he was seeking the company of a
popular white prostitute by the same name. This was 1957.
Uncle Dave was thrown in jail.

His life had been one long hardship. His weathered
skin made him look at least ten years older than Mama,
though they were but two years apart. We learned that
he'd spent his entire adulthood running, or, as he put it,
traveling from farm town to farm town as a migrant
worker. Now, cryptically, here he stood at our front door
after enduring a daylong Greyhound bus ride. As though
a circumscribed compass deep in his soul somehow set out
to unite him with the only family he really knew. The
only human being on earth who knew both his torment
and his tormentor. Understandably, Uncle Dave's errant
lifestyle did little to thwart the demons living inside
him. Drugs didn't help, neither prescribed schizophrenic
medicines or his own pharmaceutical experiments. Uncle
amused himself by periodically singing that old German
hip-hop tune about riding the white horse.

It was wrong of me to laugh, but he had this infectious
grin when he sang it that just cracked me up. The levity
didn't last very long. Shortly after our chuckles, Uncle
Dave would turn serious and argumentative. Not toward
me. Not toward anyone in particular. No one visible, at

least. "Shut up! Get away from me!" he'd yell. I laughed at first—guessing the bursts were part of some inside joke. Yeah, they were inside jokes all right. Inside the paranoid anxiety disorders knocking around his head for much of his life.

Mama and her sisters decided that Uncle Dave should go down South to live so he could have privacy and a bit of supervision at the same time. He traveled to Macon and took up residence in a trailer set on Aunt Francis's property. It's no one's fault. He was a grown man. No one could force him to take his meds. And Uncle Dave got scary when he got angry—which was often, since voices in his head were difficult to quiet. Plus, he was convinced someone was out to kill him and take his money—though he was, by all accounts, broke as a doornail.

Mama has a picture in her living room. Its frame holds a smiling Uncle Dave surrounded by her, Aunt Johnnie Bea, Aunt Annie Bell, and Aunt Francis—five senior citizens grinning like children. That photo is the only time Mama had all her siblings in one place, in one embrace. Something most of us take for granted was for her a Big Moment. All those years of pain and sorrow had disappeared, at least for that camera's flash second.

CHAPTER TWENTY

One Nation
under a Groove

Given everything that Wilbur and Orville Wright went through to set themselves skyborne more than a century ago, I would never have guessed what I was in for. Let me tell you, the U.S. airline industry makes it challenging (and expensive) to travel to godforsaken places. Macon, Mississippi, has no airport. We would need to fly into Columbus, about a thirty-minute drive away. A direct flight is, of course, out of the question. But Newark-to-Macon is also one of those routes that offer very few itinerary options. The kids and I were to fly into Atlanta's Hartsfield-Jackson Airport, arriving at about 5:30 P.M. From there, we would lay over about an hour and a half— long enough, I figured, to get a light snack and give Cole ample time to work off some energy, running in and out of those tram cars. Barring any crazy delay, with door-to-door travel time of roughly seven hours, we'd get to our peeps by around 8:00 P.M.

They'd probably never admit it, but I believe even the girls—blasé teens, nowadays—were excited about this adventure. Mama had requested the pleasure of our company at an impromptu family reunion her siblings decided to throw. My sister, whose corporate HR skills sometimes spill outside her nine-to-five, officiously pointed out that this Macon shindig had no opening reception or formal program. I'm not sure where she got her sudden wealth of knowledge on family reunion format and etiquette. It's not like we attended this sort of thing regularly. We're not black folk of the custom-made-family-T-shirt-wearing variety. She was likely using my dad's side as a gauge. They do it big, with a Gault Family Reunion Facebook page, websites, chairmen, planning committees, and everything. I have a cousin who almost makes a part-time job out of unearthing Gault historical facts. About fifteen years ago, Dad came home from one of the reunions with all kinds of archival bric-a-brac, including a U.S. Census report dating back to the 1800s. It's all quite impressive. My siblings and I get the invites in the mail, along with hotel room information, maps, schedules, a list of speakers—even off-site excursions. We just don't often go. I don't really know why. We've all gone once or twice, I think, sometime in the early nineties, for Dad's sake.

I've met a lot of Gaults on Facebook, though, and I like them; we share social media love from time to time—"liking" one another's graduations, birthdays, and other events. But to travel high and low like this sojourn to Macon? Nah. I don't know them like that. Speaking of which, my well-laid plans to fly the friendly skies for a Mississippi get-together got miserably diverted. Hurricane Arthur had other ideas.

After standing pat in Newark for roughly six hours, the kids and I finally headed southbound through a raging storm of rain and wind, checked into an Atlanta hotel around midnight, and got into Mississippi at 3:00 the next day. I will spare you the harrowing details—mostly because the flashbacks might trigger the PTSD tic I developed en route. It was a cool adventure for the kids, all three alternately cranky and punchy. On the bright side, our unexpected Atlanta visit brought a new understanding and perspective on the—how you say, culture—represented on shows like *Love & Hip Hop* and those Big Peach Housewives.

More than twenty-four hours after pulling out of our driveway in New Jersey, we were greeted in Columbus by my sister—who'd arrived with Mama the day before—along with a cousin, Fay, riding shotgun so we wouldn't get lost.

The half-hour drive along the highway was pretty

remarkable. It wasn't beautiful or majestic in the classic sense. I was blown away by the vast breadth of barren space. Seriously. Buffalo has forgotten smokestacks and factories. New Jersey has a building crammed into every square mile. Here, there were no buildings, no bridges, no big-box retailers, no office headquarters. Nothing. Coming from a landscape mauled by malls, industrial complexes, factories, cineplexes, and superstores, it was as though we were Lewis and Clark setting eyes on shore for the first time in years. There was *land* everywhere. Just hanging out and being land purely for land's sake. It was open, undeveloped, clean, unspoiled, tranquil, fresh, and unfettered rolling terrain . . . just happy to *be*.

The blank landscape did not strike my kids with the same level of wonder as it did me. They found it a little creepy. "Awkward?" they'd say. After fifteen miles or so, even the back-home novelty of cattle dotting the fields grew boring. Mama had to say, "Look, kids . . . horses!" a few too many times to catch their attention. Cole, especially, just wanted to be in Macon already.

Our highway excursion was not without entertainment value, though. Fay—my second or third cousin by marriage, I believe—has so much personality, she should have her own show. Even her stories had stories. I won't lie, I didn't manage to catch or keep track of all of them. But from what I was able to make out, her brother made a living around these parts "huntin' coon." He doesn't eat it himself, but he can "catch coon, skin coon, and sell coon" real good. And apparently there is a healthy market for what I always thought of as a higher form of rodent. What did I know? Turns out you can parboil coon, bake coon, fry coon, and serve it up with sweet potatoes. Of course, it purportedly tastes "just like chicken."

Fay's stories were mesmerizing to me. Her speech was a tinge country in the most charming way. We had nothing but time on our hands, as far as I could tell. Although we were a day late, there was no formal setup to the reunion, so it was all good. I'd always known deep down that Mama's side was where we got our flavor. You know, like that kicking cayenne spice that makes Popeyes chicken bona fide and different from all other fast-food fowl?

And had anyone gotten a peek at the Macon party, they'd say, "You ain't never lied!" When we finally crossed onto the road leading to my auntie's, I was surprisingly a little verklempt. Memories came flooding back—so fast and forceful that they were held hostage in my throat. I wanted to cry but no noise, no water released itself. I remembered this road—a far lovelier road than the one inside my recollections—paved, too. I felt a mixture of pride and triumph. Years ago, my uncle Sol struggled to hold his head up high in this rusty town. Today, for a stretch of at least ten miles or so, all the land on either side of the road belonged to him and my other family members. Every square inch. At the corner of one of the roads even stood an official street sign bearing his name. How 'bout that? This is that real-life George and Weezy Jefferson (*"took a whole lot of trying . . . just to get up that hill"*) kind of progress.

When we pulled up to the house of my late aunt Francis, my cousin Shad was one of the first people I saw. Tall, wiry thin, and dressed in a white suit. Did I mention it was a backyard cookout where everybody else had on jeans? He later reappeared wearing a different ensemble— in fact, there were three or four wardrobe changes. Maybe since he was also sort of in charge of the music, or at least the main one dancing, the outfits were choreographed to match the playlist. For example, when Swag District's "Teach Me How to Dougie" came on, it only made sense that Shad would have made the necessary transition from his burgundy-colored suit to his green slacks and multi-colored T-shirt. The soundtrack for the day included an eclectic mix of Prince (*"I ain't got no money . . . I ain't like those other guys you hang around"*), Teddy Pendergrass (*"You can't hide from yourself . . . Everywhere you go, there you are"*) and a lowdown bluesy number I'd never heard that sent Shad to writhing on the ground. He had moves like Jagger—and then some. The wormy get-down thing he was working, I came to learn, was a well-known segue in his repertoire. It was a dance one of my "just met" cousins informed me, shaking her head in mild disapproval, "he be doing in the club down here . . . just like he doing now."

Not one of my Macon relatives appeared the least bit fazed by Shad's antics. His brother, Bunt, whose name I'd learned would be traditionally pronounced "Bernard," didn't even blink. He relocated many years ago to Michigan, but it was clear that Macon was home. Everyone's attention was fixed on Mama—and, by extension, us. They were hugging and loving on her like biscuits sopping pot liquor—a "new" delicacy I'd sampled down South, with my no-meat-eating self. The shower of affection was equal parts touching and strange. I'd never seen Mama fussed over like that before. For a minute, it looked as though Bobbie might bow down and rub her corns even. If I die tomorrow, I do believe, the joy on Mama's face that day would fill my heart with everlasting peace.

It was definitely a moment—with Cousin Shad running a close second. It's not like I found him funny, like ha-ha. Or funny strange. It was more so struck by how free he was. Moving, dancing with no inhibition whatsoever. I liked that. Probably that's what family is for. To make you free.

Several of my "just met" cousins blended together in one face. I've forgotten some of their names. But that's not to understate their importance, because in their eyes and noses I found a new appreciation of my own. Ever watched those specials on TV where adoptees finally meet their birth mothers? It was like that in a way. Finally a physical connection to Mama's tribe. Her nation. Aunt Annie Bell looked like Mama in a way I never saw nearly forty years ago. Mama's namesake and I reconnected. She and I are more alike than I'd have ever guessed. She'd come down from northern Virginia. I caught her studying my face a few times when I didn't think anyone was looking. On each occasion she'd burst out laughing and say, "Girl, don't you know you in the country now!"

How did she know what I was thinking, and how did she know she could tease me like that? That's family, I guess. A bunch of cousins were going plum picking later, she said. Again, noting the quizzical hesitance written on my face, she quickly added, "Just come on!" My cousin Keesha would be going too. I'd actually met Keesha three or four years ago in New York. She'd learned she had a cousin in the Big Apple and called to introduce herself during her travels in and out of the city. Since then, we always made time for a quick visit when she blew into town. Okay, it was a total of three times. But still, we have gotten to know each other. Although she is fully grown and in her thirties I take an almost maternal pride in her accomplishments—former professor in Thailand and now a dean at a university in Ohio. We were all so tickled to be together, there was no room for anything but love.

Meanwhile, Shad was jamming. But when George Clinton's "Atomic Dog" was cued (*"Why must I be like that? Why must I chase the cat? It's the dog in me . . ."*) I thought it best the kids and I turn our attention away from the dance area, if you know what I'm saying. I feared Shad might sho' 'nuff turn it out and there'd be nothing G-rated about it.

We had plenty to hold our attention. My second (or third) cousin Charles—son of Fineness—from St. Louis had arrived with his grandson, a teenager who looked like a tall, fine version of rapper Lil' Bow Wow. He eagerly shared his phone video of Shad's dancing with Chloe, Trinity, and Cole, his "just met" cousins, lest any hump or grind were to go undocumented. Cousin Charles, I think, reminded me of his dad—whom I'd met as a little girl. Or maybe I just wanted to see a resemblance. In any case, he was youthful and solidly built and smiled with the prettiest teeth I'd ever seen; against his smooth dark skin they sparkled like white Chiclets.

Just when I thought he could beam no brighter, he took Cole's hand in his. "What's your name, young man?"

Never shy or the least bit reserved, my son proudly responded: "I'm Cole," to which Cousin Charles grew wide-eyed with excitement. He looked at Cole, looked up at me, then repeated the back-and-forth head movement. "That's my name. My last name is Cole. Did you know that?"

"Of course!" My baby laughed flippantly. Incidentally, my child tends toward very precise and loud articulation. It's his natural way of talking; I don't know where he gets it. We all get a kick out of it back home because it renders a comic twist to most everything he says. But set against this countrified backdrop, his deliberate speech seemed to ring with a pinch of Urkel-ness to the ear. Very proud and oratorical, he adds, "Because we're family. My name, *C-O-L-E*, is from the family." Cousin Charles looked like he was about to bust open. All he could do was laugh—head thrown back, Chiclets lighted and bouncing off the midday sun. "You named him that?" he asked me incredulously. I nodded. "Liza, Liza . . . Bless da Lawd!" he exclaimed. Somewhere around that point, I do believe he fell madly, deeply in love with his newfound relation. This despite the fact that, as the day wore on, Cole got more mannish than he had a right to. When Cousin Charles started playing Bible trivia that afternoon, for example, Cole had the nerve to say something like, "I thought games were supposed to be fun!" I was mortified; the only reason I didn't fall out and die is because I'm guessing (hoping, more like it) everyone assumed the sass was a function of the child's brash northern sensibilities.

The next day's events, though, showed me that my

brood and me got our personalities honestly. With much fanfare, Mama had organized an impromptu visit to her mother's baby sister and only surviving sibling, Aunt Al-Curtis. She lived just up the road a piece (country talk is highly contagious; I picked mine up in only a few hours' time). We hurriedly piled into two cars, because Aunt AlCurtis reportedly goes to bed at seven P.M. each evening. As you might imagine, she was quite feeble. But she looked very happy to see us all. Mama had said she was 93. But I'd guess she was more like 137 or thereabouts. You know most women don't like to reveal their real ages. God bless Aunt AlCurtis. She could not hear or comprehend a lick of what was going on.

Cousin Charles made all the necessary introductions, explaining to Auntie who was who by way of whom and whatnot. She smiled blankly, bless her heart. We all took seats and sat clumsily for a very pregnant five minutes or so. Looking at Auntie AlCurtis, then at one another. Then once more. "Well, this is gonna be one good time," Cousin Charles bellowed, sounding like a seventy-year-old version of Cole. He turned to Aunt AlCurtis and said, "You don't have the slightest idea who any of us are, do you? Why, of course you don't." Then he threw up his hands and let out a big sigh. On the exhale, he huffed: "Liza, Liza . . . Bless da LAWD!" It was, I think, his way of saying "my goodness" or some such. I later found out the phrase came from a 1913 poem by Paul Laurence Dunbar—one of the first African American writers to gain national acclaim, winning praise from the *New York Times* and *Harper's Weekly*. I swear if he recited the phrase once, he said it a dozen times that day.

More Bible trivia ensued, with Cousin Charles offering twenty-dollar prizes for the most obscure facts imaginable. "Name two sets of twins from the Bible," he said. "And I bet' not see a smartphone!" Cole sighed audibly and mumbled, "Oh, goodness gracious!"—surely removing all doubt of his questionable home training. All I could do was laugh. And not just a quiet snicker. This laughing fit was not a good look. As awkward moments are prone to do for me, reflexive giggles flowed in huge waves—the spigot irretrievably unplugged. I feared I might wet my pants at any moment.

Meanwhile, Mama seemed to be under the misguided impression that she and Aunt AlCurtis were actually engaged in a conversation. I heard her say, "Vanilla's daughter" at least a half dozen times. You gotta love Mama's can-do spirit. She gives up on nothing, that woman. I had to fight back tears—from all the laughing. Although Mama's moment with her mother's sister was awfully touching, Cousin Charles had that look on his face that said (in a sick and tired way), "Liza. Liza. Bless da Lawd."

And my sister, who somehow seemed to have a memo of

everywhere we were supposed to go and when, signaled that our visit with Auntie Hard-of-Hearing was drawing toward its close.

We were on a tight schedule, for sure, trying to squeeze nearly a lifetime of living into just forty-eight hours. Yet my visit never felt the least bit frenetic or rushed. I had the time to enjoy good food. No one believes this, but there were witnesses when I ate *four*—count 'em—helpings of fried fish and coleslaw. The kids and I did, indeed, go plum picking. My cousin drove along a very long and winding road that had no street signs, just bends along the way that she instinctively knew how and when to navigate. I wondered whose plums we were picking. But Keesha told me that according to Aunt Bell, "Everybody up yonder is yo' kin."

Afterward, although it was a couple of miles out of the way, my cousin took me by a long-forgotten, modest structure on the edges of Macon. New Hope United Methodist Church was more of a hut-looking white clapboard building, as I recall. When my siblings and I visited back in the seventies, Aunt Annie Bell had us there every Sunday. We'd walk up the weather-beaten stairs in the morning—and often return later in the day. Back then the church-yard outdoor part was tented and done up for revival meetings. I remember good singing. Auntie and the rest of the congregants didn't do a lot of Holy Ghost dancing or falling out. But they were caught up in the Spirit just enough to distract them while we horsed around, turning the grounds into our own slapdash playground.

Today, New Hope is pretty and manicured. The wobbly old wooden church I recall has been replaced by a modern brick building that is almost elegant. And I'm seeing something I missed on the long-ago "playground," the reason my cousin drove here in the first place. A small cemetery, with maybe a couple dozen plots. A large tombstone just about centers the narrow parcel. In grand, etched lettering *COLES* is centered along its front. One side reads: *JOHNNIE 1883–1953*, and the other side says *ANNIE BELL 1881–1961*. And just a few feet away: *VANILLA COLE Dec. 24, 1903–Jan. 12, 1937*. I was staring at the place where Mama's mother lay. A piece of my soul sharing the same air with a piece of hers. Johnnie and Annie Bell, I assume, were my great-grandparents. They must've had love for one another, because here they lay eternally side by side. Somewhere in my life, two married folks in my bloodline must have gotten it right. My great-grands landed on that "let no man put asunder" thing, because here they were in the ever after. Together.

I'd stumbled upon something I never even knew my heart longed for.

CHAPTER TWENTY-ONE

Sho' You Right

I have always had very strong opinions and firm hunches. That makes it appear as though I know more than I really do. It's definitely a Mama thing. And, throughout my whole life, I've found it easily one of her most annoying traits.

Mama thinks she knows *Ev-er-y-thing*—about any and everything, even that which no one would have any earthly way of knowing.

She is an expert on communicable disease. The hacking stranger in the seat in front of us? "Sounds like a case of TB. Move down." A small-town Elsa Klensch, Mama has been known to forecast fall fashions. "The gaucho pant is coming back, baby. Believe me when I tell you." When my kids were babies, she took to prescribing treatments from six hundred miles away. "Put some Vicks VapoRub all over that baby and wrap him in a towel." If the Federal Bureau of Investigation had only thought to ask her, "Excuse us, ma'am. Do you know where Teamster boss Jimmy Hoffa might be?" Mama wouldn't flinch or stammer. She'd say with absolute certainty, "That fool crook? My sister Lucille saw him driving a beat-up Brougham on 8 Mile and Van Dyke. He always did love him some *DEE*troit floozies."

I can see why Mama took to unraveling the world's mysteries by her own self. Life is hard. Life is full of questions. I would be remiss—and a whole lot of folks would talk bad about me—if I were to leave the obvious unsaid: I can be a bit of a know-it-all too. (At least that's what "they" say.) That's the irony of my magazine shtick. From interviewing some clinical psychologists, parsing research studies, writing online posts, and talking to lots of other moms, I sometimes get asked to appear on TV and radio programs. They introduce me as a "parenting expert." Funny. Right? In the great scheme of things, I'm not an expert on jack. But I do know what I know that I know.

And even in the middle of my crazy, I can usually hold on to a small piece of that knowing. We've all heard the saying, "If Mama ain't happy . . ." (you know the rest). It makes perfect sense, but what lies underneath that adage is seldom spoken: "Mama's gotta make herself happy . . . first." By any means necessary.

A friend recently tried to explain the rationale of buying an at-home spinning bike on eBay—and even went so far as to tape the gym instructor's sessions on an iPad. The demands of three-year-old twins were making it next to impossible to make it to the gym. I marveled at two things: this parent's ingenuity, first and foremost. I never thought to actually record my favorite teacher's playlist and class drills. Maybe it's the writer in me; feels a bit like copyright infringement. But, anyhoo. The other part of this elaborate (and pricey) endeavor saddened me and got me to thinking, "Talk about desperate!"

We've all been there, though—at that point at which the pint-sized creatures we love and care for completely take over our lives. Like the plotline of a low-budget sci-fi flick, they sneak in, then slowly creep through everything— invade our business and professional lives, bedrooms and bank accounts. It's been a minute, but I was there years ago. Sort of.

Here's where some might question my maternal judgment. Others might question my morals. But I remember when my kids were little and I was fiending for a workout— and not just any workout, but Andrea's "Cardio-Box & Sculpt" at the Y—the crumb snatchers came with me. I packed bags with their favorite treats, board books, crayons, and crafts. And they sat alongside the gym while their mama got her groove on. It was, perhaps, not ideal that their young impressionable heads were being filled with

Fitty Cent blaring in the background, spitting verses like: "You can find me in club, bottle full of bub." But, hey, life is not perfect.

Probably their friends' moms were not in the middle of a room packed with sweaty men and women yelling, "Awww, yeah! That's my jam!" But the way I figure, it was in some ways a teachable moment: This caregiver person charged with supplying our every need is actually a multi-faceted whole person. Okay, maybe they didn't go that deep with their analysis. But at the very least, it brought some small things to light: On occasion, Mommy can still drop it like it's hot. I've never seen a research study on the subject, but I am confident that knowledge is valuable to their overall well-being.

The girls, especially, have to see me doing me. As they were seated on the gym floor—nestled between the booming bass of the speakers—at first I wrestled with a small amount of guilt. While I am, indeed, very proud of my inner gangster, I was not likely to win a Mother of the Year Award belting alongside Missy Elliott, *"Getcha freak on . . . Getcha freak on . . . Getcha, getcha, getcha freak on!"*

I thought long and hard about the ramifications of my actions. Well, admittedly by *long and hard* I'm saying I thought about it the whole time I was changing into my gym clothes—concluding that the upside outweighed any potential dangers. It's not like I was dragging my babies to a crack house, for goodness' sake. And just think how much nicer and much more patient a mom I would be after my fix.

Over the years, I'd written or edited at least a dozen twists on the same tired "Me Time" schtick . . . "Grab Some Me Time in No Time." "How to Sneak In Me Time." "5 Steps to Guilt-Free Me Time." Each tip said pretty much the same thing: Call a girlfriend, get a mani-pedi, soak in a tub of lavender oils. Bump all that nonsense! I'm grown. I shouldn't have to pencil in a bath. And, in case you don't know, gossip is best served fresh. I can't be like, "Girl, we gon' spill some tea a week from Tuesday at three." Maybe I'm wrong. Call me a bad mother. But I just think that if you need somebody to tell you when and how to take care of yourself, you don't need Me Time. You need Jesus!

If you promise not to put me on blast, I'll tell you a little secret. My ultimate Me Time fix involves a simple little flip of the switch I do in my head from time to time. It's handy-dandy and needs no scheduling, planning, or calling in favors. Normally, I don't share this with just anybody. But I sense we are starting to feel each other right about now. My trick has become second nature for me, as I've had years of practice. For some of you, it might take regular and concerted effort. Here goes:

When various and sundry people get in your ear—kids,

spouses, coworkers, family—about their needs and wants, pay them no mind. Repeat as needed.

It's nice if you manage to smile or look halfway engaged while you tune folks out. Again, I'm very accomplished in this area. For you, it may take some work. My recommendation is that this tack be practiced at least three times a day. But I leave that up to individual discretion. Maybe it's just the way I'm wired, but some days I need these momentary periods of checking out just to maintain my sanity. Is it right? I'm not sure. But it works for me.

The more living I'm blessed to have on this earth, the more obvious it is that I am in control of very little. I've learned that sometimes, even with lots of consideration, firm answers are hard to come by. You gotta go for what you know. When I step back and look at my kids, I remember being in the room when they were made. But at the same time, I know without a doubt that they are products of a force far more powerful than I. Their intricate personalities. The extraordinary workings of their minds. And, of course, their heart-stopping beauty. As a mere human being, I had no real hand in their creation. I was just the vessel chosen to bring them here. So why am I tripping? Acting as though by following this or that course of action, I can "make" them into the people they should be? News flash, people: Our kids are already who they're supposed to be! Now that I am an older mom, I realize how important it is to be like the immortal James Brown when he said, "I'm ready to get up and do *my* thang."

The parenting machine would have us thinking that we wield some superhero powers to retool our rug rats into creatures of our own design. That's ludicrous and tiring. I refuse to go out like that. All I need is some confidence in my own ability and faith in the man upstairs. I can fill them up with enough love and righteousness to keep them safe and strong. I do my very best. But when I fail—and, Lord knows, I often do—there is grace. Of that I'm sure. Grace is a concept I think I came to understand in my late teens or so. I can recall a point where Mama seemed to recognize that I was a bit too old for beatdowns—physical or verbal. I used to think I'd simply worn her down, seeing as I was the last child in the house and she was probably tiring of the same old adolescent hijinks. But in hindsight I can see now that she was trying to help me grow into the woman I needed to be. Whenever I displayed some kind of questionable behavior, instead of yelling, she'd pause for what felt like an hour. These were rare occasions on which Mama did not have the answer and didn't front like there even was one. Times when she did not reach back and grab a catchy country phrase as a healing balm on life's challenges.

I could sense her concern and in her eyes it was clear that the worry was sometimes laced with a scant trace of equal parts confusion and disapproval—like, "Don't you remember how I raised you?" She was trying to save me from myself in those moments. And the silence was deafening. Then, after seemingly staring clear through my body's every cellular membrane, she would sigh and softly say: "Slow your roll, baby girl. Slow your roll." It's that time now—to take it back there.

To Chloe, Trinity, and Cole:
You rock my world

Acknowledgments

Since my name appears on the cover and this book is all about me, my mama, and my kids—you probably think I simply thought it up and started finger dancing on my keyboard. Not even. *Child, Please* would not exist without the genius, encouragement, and gentle prodding of Pitchapalooza's Arielle Eckstut and David Henry Sterry. You guys are the truth! Thank you, Arielle, for hooking me up with the best agent in the industry, Jim Levine. Seriously. You had faith in my work from the get-go and will always be my fairy godfather. Nothing but grace led me to Tarcher and the expert hands of Sara Carder, my editor and confidante. I have no doubt that Sara, her assistant, Joanna Ng, and Keely Platte have won a "Do Not Pass Go" card to heaven after putting up with me. Mere words don't come close to expressing the love gratitude I have for my mama. Not just for the usual stuff like giving me life, raising me up, and so on. Essie Mae has been a rock star throughout this (sometimes difficult) memoir process; her grace, humility, and generosity shouldn't have surprised me but kinda did. I am also blessed with the best brother and sister a girl could wish for. My Ace Boons, Faren, and Anthony, lavish me with more love and attention than I have a right to. I've also been embraced by a tight extended family; they always catch me when I fall. Two summers ago, Saade and Alan Berkowitz gave me a soft place to land when I needed it most. Special thank-you's to my bedrocks: Vanessa Monroe, Tanya Carter, Patrik Henry Bass, Monique Greenwood, Carmen Jackson, Letena Lindsay, Gina Paige, Mary Ann D'Urso, Pamela Edwards Christiani, Cherlynn Miller, Tanya Poole Hughes, and my spiritual mama, Deaconess Ann Brown. Last, but certainly not least, shout-outs to the Glam Team: Keith Major, Lysette Drumgold, Sherwin Jones, and Penny Wang.

If you enjoyed this book, visit

www.tarcherbooks.com

and sign up for Tarcher's e-newsletter to receive
special offers, giveaway promotions, and
information on hot upcoming releases.

TARCHER
PENGUIN

Great Lives Begin with Great Ideas

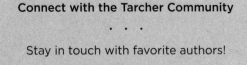

Connect with the Tarcher Community

• • •

Stay in touch with favorite authors!
Enter weekly contests!
Read exclusive excerpts!
Voice your opinions!

Follow us

 Tarcher Books

@TarcherBooks

If you would like to place a bulk order
of this book, call 1-800-847-5515.